PR IN PRACTICE SERIES

Online
Public
Relations

David Phillips

the Institute *of* Public Relations

**KOGAN
PAGE**

First published in 2001

Kogan Page Limited
120 Pentonville Road
London N1 9JN
UK

Kogan Page US
22 Broad Street
Milford CT 06460
USA

British Library Cataloguing in Publication Data

A CIP record for this book is available from the British Library.

ISBN 0 7494 3510 0

Typeset by Jean Cussons Typesetting, Diss, Norfolk
Printed and bound by Creative Print and Design (Wales) Ebbw Vale

Contents

List of figures

Foreword

Without doubt, the Internet age has arrived. With it has arrived a revolution in public relations. This revolution not only involves the way we communicate, but the nature of communication itself.

In this book on e-public relations, David Phillips shows how the Internet is revolutionizing the role and work of the PR professional. The book is not for those who wish to learn the mechanics of how to construct a Web site or how to set up a virtual press office. It is about how to use this potent and energizing medium intelligently and effectively.

Much has been written on the Internet as just another channel of communication. Nothing could be further from the truth. The Internet is a channel of communication, but it is much more than that. Its unique properties of reach and richness have transformed the quality of communication. Furthermore, the nature of Internet publics, or communities, is quite different from those that have been traditionally the domain of the PR practitioner.

Starting with an explanation of the Internet and then describing how it can be used, David Phillips provides an overview of the new communication environment and its potential. He then goes on to explore how an organization can establish a presence on the Internet and how the various Internet communities can be engaged using the variety of channels offered by the new media.

Of vital interest are the topics of reputation and issues management on the Internet. David Phillips explores how reputations can be destroyed or enhanced depending on how Internet relationships are managed and he also provides similar advice on managing issues as they arise. The anti-capitalist protests in Seattle, London and Stockholm have been extensively organized and promoted via the Internet and it is apparent that activist groups will use the medium increasingly. This of course provides a great opportunity as well as being a potential threat for PR professionals who are the guardians of organizational reputation.

The Internet within an internal communications context is also discussed: its uses, abuses and how to harness its power effectively.

Rounded off with an overview of the legal implications of Internet activity and a look into the future, this book provides a timely and authoritative overview of e-PR. It provides some clear pointers for organizing PR professionally now and indicates a vision of the future. Any PR professional wanting to conduct his or her business in the modern interconnected world will regard this book as a must.

Anne Gregory
Series Editor

Preface

This book has been written to help PR practitioners.

The Internet affects all forms of PR practice and yet there are very few books or guides for the PR industry. There is a lot of confusion. Levels of competence range from excellence to almost complete ignorance; this makes 'pitching' the content of this book difficult.

No attempt has been made to cater for the complete 'newbie'. For such people, a favourite nephew or niece will be a better resource for information. Their enthusiasm when showing you round the Internet will make the experience an absolute joy and much less daunting than the local library or Chamber of Commerce.

Many people see the Internet as a complicated technology. But the instructions book is very small. A friend, when asked to explain how to use the Internet, reduced its instructions to:

On a Web page, if a word is blue and underlined 'click' on it.
To receive e-mail click on the bold type in the 'in box'.
To join a chat group click 'Chat'.
To get really scared type in your credit card number.
To be reassured tell everyone you did it at a party and find that it's really quite safe.
And, to be really impressed, buy a book from a Web site.
It's all very easy.

These instructions need lots of practice.

You may have to go a little further to get the best from this book. Surf a little, send a few e-mails, and try instant messaging or a chat room. Get to know the language of the Internet. Talk to friends and read Internet columns in good old-fashioned newspapers. Then put on your professional PR hat.

Internet PR has two elements. The first is in seeking, learning and applying the best practice of the day and the second is in constant re-evaluation, re-learning fast, evolving offline and online practice. There is information here that you may not want to use in practice and there is technology that, though described in some detail, will baffle you. Don't be put off. In the next office, just down the street or in the gym is someone who is an expert. Not an expert on everything and not necessarily an expert in PR, but who has tried out some aspect that is beyond your experience. If after that you are desperate to know how to do something, go to the biggest library you know, the Internet.

No one is an expert on all the many aspects of the Internet as it affects existing, let alone emerging, PR practice. This book attempts to show best practice as far as it is known. It is up to you as to the depth of detail and implementation that is suited to your practice or organization but here, at least, is a set of rules that will point you in the right direction.

There are five rules to start you off:

1. Ask questions.
2. Don't experiment on your organization/client; try it yourself first.
3. Play safe with your organization/client.
4. Invest time in understanding the opportunities.
5. Be ethical in everything you do.

The next few pages are terribly serious, while the Internet is largely about fun, interaction and community. So when you turn the last page, go somewhere that you believe the Internet has no influence and kick over the traces and then return to work, apply some of its ideas and hang on for the ride of your life.

Acknowledgements

In the four weeks taken to write this book, Margaret, my wife, has been wonderful – not that I have been distant but perhaps less than homely. It takes some considerable understanding to live in a house when one of the inhabitants says not a word for 14 hours a day!

Anne Gregory, the editor of this series, has been a hero. She gave me a free hand, a lot of advice, bucket loads of encouragement and shared her considerable wisdom and knowledge of both PR and the Internet.

Alison Clark, one of the truly excellent thinkers in the realm of Internet PR, not only provided support and criticism, she allowed me to use much of her thinking and knowledge in these pages. This is a gift of two halves. Living up to her level of thinking and knowledge is hard. Being able to include it in the text is wonderful.

Roy Lipski and Mark Adams, with their knowledge of what happens across the Internet and its influence on organizations and people, have endlessly made me review best practice in the light of experience, and Bill Comcowich, with massive experience on the other side of the Atlantic, was free with criticism and his knowledge. Shel Holtz, whose excellent book *Public Relations on the Net* (Amacon) and his excellent discussion list (see www.holtz.com), among others, has also been a source of excellent information and real practical PR experience for the Internet age.

Finally, there are some hundreds of contributors, too many to thank individually, who have shared their experiences and knowledge in discussion lists, Web pages and books to ensure that these pages are reasonably comprehensive and germane to current day practice.

To all, my thanks.

Introduction

> Our role in advocacy will be from the heart of the board decision and will be a marked asset if it is stratospherically above the role of benighted spin-doctor.[1]

The Internet has matured to the extent that its users expect professionalism. This book is intended to help practitioners develop such excellence. It is not intended to be a book on 'How to do Internet Public Relations'. That is up to the individual practitioner applying traditional PR principles and skills. There are excellent authors and many online discussions and publications that will keep these subjects fresh and also provide examples of PR using the Internet.

The Internet offers great opportunities to deploy the creative spark found by lightly scratching members of this profession. There are many guidance notes that can be applied to such creativity and deployed to help you deliver better PR in the Internet-enabled era.

Just by sending an e-mail, every practitioner, who only months ago worked in a region or country, is now practising on a world stage, although many have yet to find this out. It is an exhilarating time and none more so than for PR as a whole.

---

[1] David Phillips, to the Institute of Public Relations National Conference, 1995

INFORMATION AND COMMUNICATION TECHNOLOGIES FOR PR

The earliest known information and communications technologies (ICT) paper to any PR audience was given by me. It was called 'New PR' and presented to the Institute of Public Relations Millennium Force Symposium, Stratford on Avon, UK. It is available at: http://www.fsvo.com/netreputation/newpr.

The Internet's capability to make available data, information and knowledge is prodigious. The amount of information available about the tiniest company or mightiest government department goes way beyond their respective Web sites or employees' e-mail contacts. Today, a huge and growing range of Internet-enabled agencies, people and 'news' outlets provide endless online detail mostly without the knowledge of the organizations involved.

The Internet audiences are huge, questioning and inquisitive. Internet applications are easy to use and fun. This is why over a quarter of the population use Internet technologies and why it is so attractive to organizations. Local and global interest in our organizations offers tremendous social and cultural as well as marketing opportunities. Ease of communication makes business relationships much more efficient, cuts time and cost and speeds trade. This means that the Internet has the potential to hold immense power over relationships and reputations for every organization.

Discrepancies in information bring about loss of confidence, trust, reputation and breakdown in relationships. When this happens to an organization, it foregoes the potential to benefit from the advantages available because of the Internet.

The Institute of Public Relations report on the work and research of the UK PR industry Internet Commission is entitled 'The Death of Spin'. The reason for this title is very germane. 'Spin' wherever practised inevitably finds its way into the information-hungry Internet and is thereafter a threat to relationships, a hidden canker and latent threat to the survival of the organization. Untruths, half-truths and extravagant claims become a reputation time bomb. This is why organizations and practitioners need to apply professional, ethical PR discipline to relationship management both online and offline. Internet PR is not a bolt-on, nice-to-have option: it is critical to survival.

There are many ways an organization's PR practitioner will communicate using Internet technologies. A number of the currently relevant ones are explored in some depth in this book. But the Internet also brings PR closer to the heart of corporate re-engineering, corporate governance, corporate and brand relationships, reputation promotion and issues management. This is a great opportunity.

What will rapidly become apparent is that there are very few, if any, methods for communication that are the exclusive domain of the PR practitioner. Today, the Internet has put communications tools and techniques, once the unique advantage of a few professions, into the hands of everyone with a modem and a computer. The concepts of one-to-one, one-to-many and many-to-many, laid down in 'New PR' are very important to modern PR practice.

Anyone can create a Web site, use e-mail or instant messages (IM) and discuss issues of the day in newsgroups and on bulletin boards. Millions of people upload and download pictures and video every day to the delight of admiring grandparents, friends, relatives and the world at large. This is not a PR, corporate or media tycoon's prerogative.

The press officer is no longer the only means for access by a journalist. Corporate information is available on company, government, media, academic and personal Web sites and no longer exclusive to corporate brochures and analysts' briefings. Political campaigns are driven by wide-ranging, informed and (even globally) connected constituents. Financial performance, even the level of commitment to vendors and commercial partners, is wide open to scrutiny and well beyond the control once exercised behind the mahogany door of the corporate affairs director.

Rather, it becomes apparent, it is PR skills that need to be transferred to stakeholders throughout the organization. There is a responsibility to e-enable and automate to become more efficient and facilitate, create and promote the framework for advantageous enterprise-wide relationships with the organization's constituency. This means that the raw materials for communication need to be collected, authenticated and made available. This is a knowledge management activity (a subject in its own right). It requires internal and external resources to be acquired in a structured way.

Knowledge of and access to delivery platforms and interoperation with channels for communication are also important.

Practitioners have a choice. They can be in the centre of providing reliable Internet resources or they will have to use services provided by another department. As providers of much of the most visible communication in cyberspace, it is important that sources are the best and the most reliable when used by PR practitioners.

Because information can flow freely round an organization, the person or department with the best resource will, de facto, become the most accepted and used author. Knowledge will truly be the representative of power.

1

Internet public relations

In just a few more years, the current homogenised 'voice of business' – the sound of mission statements and brochures – will seem as contrived and artificial as the language of the 18th century French Court.[1]

Internet PR ranges from the strategic management of corporate ethos to delivery of an appropriate format photograph by e-mail to a magazine journalist. At both strategic and process levels the PR rules are the same.

The process includes the need to know about the Internet constituents (eg the journalist), mutual understanding of each other's needs (eg a TIFF image of a photograph at 300 dpi), the means for delivering service using acceptable delivery platforms, channels and technologies (eg e-mail) and a clear understanding that this action offers an image to a potentially global audience (eg because most magazines publish an Internet online version – and so the journalist may also want a 75 dpi JPG image as well).

---

[1] *The Cluetrain Manifesto*, ft.com

At the strategic level, the process for delivery of a simple TIFF image has broad consequences. The TIFF image offers rich content about the organization. The image associated with a caption, without a caption and in a different context has potential to enhance or hurt the organization. Its transmission to a journalist means it is available for global distribution by any number of people and organizations as it migrates to the online version of the magazine, is potentially copied, even changed and morphed and put in other Web sites and is thereby globally available for all eternity. The range of different people who may see the image is important and so too are the many agendas that modern day, informed, global and culturally diverse publics carry with them.

The image and its associated perceptions, which stretch well beyond the control of the practitioner, can influence people such that they have active, aware and latent potential for a relationship with the organization. These people form a broad constituency. This means that the practitioner needs an understanding of the actual and potential consequences and nature of interaction arising from that, possibly remote, relationship. This is the nature of network communications. Thus the simplest processes of Internet-enabled activity undertaken in every corner of the organization and beyond the immediate control of the practitioner have very wide PR consequences for an organization and its many stakeholders.

There are four areas of management and empowerment for Internet PR. There is content, and Internet audiences appreciate rich content. There is the means by which the information is made available, namely its reach. There are the people using the Internet, namely constituents, and then there is the nature of relationships with constituents creating empathy within organizations.

RICHNESS

A simple Web site needs very little information and does not have to include lots of flashing graphics, chat rooms, hundreds of hyperlinks or dynamic interactivity. If the quality of the information is good such sites can be popular. There are compelling reasons for lots of extra twiddly bits and we will discuss them. But the basics of Web presence are the quality of information, the effort put into assuring visitors that they can trust the information and simple navigation to and within the site. Basics like spelling mistakes are a real turn-off and so elementary PR skills remain very important. Other forms of Internet richness, such as content provided to bulletin boards, discussion lists and even e-mail need similar basic care and appeal.

Most organizations will want to offer rich information. This may be made available on the Web site. It may include briefings, backgrounders, explanations, product and service information as well as entertainment and lots of fun. Richness can be almost permanently available or ephemeral. It can be based in a Web page, in an e-mail or discussion group. It may be derived from online integration of an organization's database or by providing access to third party information. It will be there competing for the time Internet users have available and all the sites they want to see.

Lots of other people will add richness to the Internet; some of it could be about your organization. They may comment on your site, link all or single pages to their Web sites or e-mails or even into chat discussions. In many cases you may never know it's there. Rich information can be provided by many people and organizations as well as your own. The practitioner will always want and need to know who and what is 'out there' in cyberspace influencing his or her organization's Internet constituents. Some of it will help, aid, assist or be included in your Web presence to enhance the richness you offer visitors.

REACH

There are billions of Web pages. Collected together they form millions of Web sites but there are only a few hundred millions of Internet users. This means that no one can visit all the available Web pages, still less read or assimilate their content. At the same time there are billions of e-mail messages and it is simply not possible for the Internet population to read them all. To make life harder, there is information buried deep in computers that will be accessed only when asked for (called 'deep Web') and that is said to multiply information available to Internet users by a factor of 500! While technology is now used to access much of this information, most people need to find what they need when they need it. The idea that a message can be 'pushed' to an audience without the absolute and individual acceptance of the recipient is arrogance beyond belief. Worse still, it upsets us all when we are spammed or have to kill endless 'pop-up' pages.

The Internet is a 'pull' form of communication. By that I mean people will seek information, action, fun and anything else when they want it and when competition for their time makes it all possible. All other Internet activity and promotion are irritants. Some argue that the new economy's currency is the attention of constituents and others argue that being an Internet navigator for people to use to find stuff in cyberspace brings wider rewards. For those of us who argue that wealth is now measured in knowledge units, both may be right.

The practitioner can aid this pull process and make it worthwhile for the user by offering advantageous exchanges across the Internet. Most people go to sites they know or use search engines. In addition they use the news and views of other Internet users (information found on a favoured Web site or from online discussion) and they use referrals from one site to the next.

Making sure that your rich content is known about in cyberspace means more people come to your site, interact with your organization, identify with other offline activities and understand your organization better. This means that you reach out to your audience via the Internet and offer the incentive for your audience to want to seek out your organization as well. Reach is at its best when each party has mutual magnetism.

CONSTITUENCY

In the past, broadcast information was beamed to complete populations. Progressively, as more media became available, information was directed to parts of the population (market sectors, publics, stakeholders). Local newspapers provided local information, national journals nationwide information.

The explosion of channels for communication in press, radio and television meant that communicators could reach sections of the population with information that was mostly, and in some cases exclusively, intended for the recipient. Most of this information spread from one public to another slowly, if at all, and often only by word of mouth.

In the Internet world everyone can see almost everything they are interested in. In looking for subject-specific information, they come across information that may have been aimed at a different narrowcast organization or group of people or even an individual; interest is aroused and wider understanding is immediately available.

Internet users choose what information they want to receive. They also choose who they will accept it from. In addition, they too can distribute information and it can be available to millions of people all over the world. People migrate towards Web sites that reflect their interests, lifestyle and concerns at the time that they choose to satisfy their immediate needs. In addition they visit discussion lists and comment on their interests and experiences with like-minded people among this global audience.

The traditional marketing and PR model that segmented the population into social, economic and market sectors and interests, does not translate well to the Internet. The interests of people are more complex than the neat boxes of interests that have been traditionally used for communication management. At once an individual can be concerned about the environment and yet buy exotic fruit flown halfway round the world. Traditional teaching about PR 'publics' has to be revised to accommodate these complex motivations. The principles laid down by Grunig, however, remain consistent for Internet relationships. His theory can be translated as follows.

When an organization or its constituents seek to affect each other they create PR issues and when these people choose to react, they can become members of a public. Publics form around issues.

The Internet constituent will readily identify a problem with an organization, its Web site, promise, service, products or even culture. In recognizing a problem, people actively seek information about the issue that concerns them. When browsing the Internet, this is easy. The user is already plugged into the world's biggest library (the Internet). They may also file away (process, bookmark, copy and paste) information that comes to them unsought.

People notice the extent to which there are obstacles that limit their ability to do things, find information, buy products or have fun. The level of a person's problem and constraint recognition will determine whether or not they are likely to seek information actively or passively. This process is made easy and fast by the functionality of the Internet.

The level of involvement with an organization's Web site, discussion, information, fancy graphic or online game shows the extent to which a person feels connected to a particular situation and will determine whether he or she is likely to act or not.

PUBLICS DEFINED

J E Grunig defined publics in his 1982 paper 'The message-attitude-behavior relationship: Communication behavior of organizations', published in *Communication Research*.[2]

He defined three types of publics and they are as relevant to the Internet as to every other form of public relations:

1. *Latent publics* are low in problem recognition and involvement. They may be affected by an issue, but are not involved in any activity concerning it.
2. *Aware publics* while high in problem recognition may be constrained in their action and involvement.
3. *Active publics* are high in problem recognition and involvement and have few constraints for action.

In 1984 Grunig and Hunt added a fourth public, non-publics, defined as having no interest in the issue.[3] Today, these people can be identified in Internet terms as those who do not have ready access to the Internet.

Though two decades have elapsed, these definitions of publics, our constituents, and what drives them, have not been bettered.

The organization, when addressing Internet audiences, may want to consider the many influences that are in play. In this book, the expression 'publics' and market segments are avoided and the broader expression 'constituents' is applied.

People using the Internet show their enthusiasm for a product, service or item of information with the click of a mouse or through online comment and debate. Online constituents are very indi-

---

[2] Grunig, J (1982) The message-attitude-behaviour relationship: communication behaviour of organisations, *Communication Research*, Vol 9, pp 163–300

[3] Grunig, J and Hunt, T (1984) *Managing Public Relations*, Holt, Rinehart and Winston, New York

vidual. The idea of a 'public of one' or 'market of one' comes into focus when imagining someone seeking information. On the one hand an individual may know the URL: www.thesitethatiwant. com, but this may only offer part of the solution because a subject search using a search engine (inside the site or across the Web) will offer a range of pages and Web sites. The answer may not be there or there may be a range of alternative resources to be evaluated. In turn these may not be reliable and so a question in a discussion group may be needed to help find an expert or expert direction to a Web site to provide a solution.

In the meantime you are preparing your Web site and are motivating your constituents so that when they seek the information that you have available and it is relevant to the seeker's need, these processes will point you out. In a networked community of networked information you can, indeed have to, appeal to a market of one.

EMPATHY

The relationship between an organization and its constituency is made or marred by mutually held needs, interests and beliefs. This is not to say that their interaction may not have a mutual influence one over the other. There is a need for understanding, compassion and sympathy for the views and interests of the Internet public in the process of building online relationships. This leads to trusting, informed and commercial as well as interactive relationships. These can enhance the benefits to both the organization and the Internet user.

Knowing the broader interests, aspirations and motivations of Internet users opens up the opportunity to develop trusted and appreciated reputations and relationships. In turn this affects the nature of information that organizations will need to make available, the areas of interest relevant and the nature of constituents. A virtuous circle is then in play. It comprises richness and content, the reach relevant for the content, the constituents relevant to the content and the close association of online (and offline) culture creating empathy to meet the needs of the constituents and the organization. In turn this understanding will influence the content and richness of content provided by the organization. This forms an endless interaction between richness, reach, constituency and

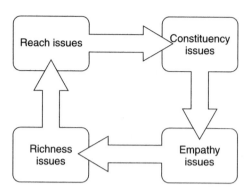

Figure 1.1 *The four areas of management and empowerment*

empathy (see Figure 1.1). This is, in its truest sense, public relations.

The practical implications of richness, reach, constituency and empathy will be explored in Chapter 8 where these factors are evaluated.

2

The Internet

The World Wide Web is the universe of network-accessible information, an embodiment of human knowledge.[1]

TOUCHING ON ALL FORMS OF COMMUNICATION

The Internet is much more than Web sites and e-mail. It influences the life of everyone. For most, the influence is indirect. Internet capability today is used to ease the flow of food to the hungry, offer holidays to the City trader, information to the scientist and fun to children. Its existing capability and awesome potential transports data, promotes products and services, enables marketing functions, offers knowledge acquisition and management and is quite capable of remotely activating computers and machines.

The Internet is a range of enabling technologies. It combines the largest resource of information ever. More new knowledge will become accessible via the Internet in the time it takes to read this book than all the written knowledge accumulated up to the Declaration of American Independence.

---

[1] Tim Berners-Lee, the inventor of the World Wide Web

One of the nice things about the Internet is that there are some really easy-to-use resources.

Internet jargon and descriptions of all things IT and Internet (in basic and understandable English) are found at: http://www.whatis.com.

The really useful backgrounder about the Internet is at Living Internet. Ten minutes here and you will be well on the way to more solutions than you thought you had needs: http://www.livinginternet.com/.

The Internet is used across many delivery platforms for communication, complementing (as well as being largely integral to production of) print, telephone, radio and television. Delivery platforms such as the humble PC, WAP phone, information kiosk, game machine, e-book, Internet-enabled Palm Pilot, IP (Internet Protocol) driven touch screen, etc, are in common use in the richer nations.

The Internet has spawned more channels for communication than the combined channels invented by mankind up to the 20th century. The channels for communication grow day by day. With e-mail, Web sites, instant messaging, chat, discussion lists, bulletin boards, interactive television (iTV), in-car navigation and information systems, the list keeps growing. Portals, vortals, marts, auctions, vertiports and further arrays of unpronounceable forms of communication appear all the time. The range of delivery platforms and channels is growing and, far from leading to convergence, is creating a wider range of choices and communications permutations. This capability means that the outflow of an organization's information, its interpretation by people and machines and the combined impact on a wide constituency affects relationships at every level throughout the world.

Where once the PR practitioner needed to know about the processes of print, presentations and exhibitions, now everyone has to be able to configure and populate (with rich meaningful content) a Web site, discussion list, chat room, AVI video, interactive e-game, e-mail and messaging. Web cam, virtual tour, online conference, SMS and WAP are additional channels for communication. The opportunities, the need for understanding and the realistic application of such facilities are now part of the stock in trade of the communicator. Anyone can do it but only the well-informed, well-disciplined and strategically capable communicator will make it meaningful.

A BRIEF BACKGROUNDER

When you use the Internet you send and receive 'packets' of information. These packets have a label attached to them saying what sort of packet they are. The first bit of information on the label says that this package is a TCP/IP (Transmission Control Protocol/Internet Protocol) piece of information and therefore belongs to the Internet.

The next piece of information shows a computer what rules the packet is using. These rules are also called protocols and are used for different forms of Internet communication; it is worth knowing just a bit about how it all works.

Cyberspace

Individuals and organizations using the Internet create a 'place' or presence in 'cyberspace'.

Information in a Web site is stored on one computer and can also be stored on more than one computer (a mirror Web site). However, the content of a Web site may be derived from information that can be held on hundreds of other computers located anywhere in the world. For example, a Web page can include a lot of links to other pages on the same Web site and held on the same computer. In addition the page can also include information from other Web pages by putting the name of that site within the page. This is called hyperlinking. It can make a very small Web site appear to be very large by using information from all over the Web.

When an individual or an organization has control of a presence or place in cyberspace it is called a 'property'. This can include one or several Web sites (and many organizations have several Internet properties). Frequently such properties are of a different nature such as a Web site and a newsgroup or chat room.

The apparent impression is that we are all completely interconnected and can communicate across the world and that information can flow freely to anyone who is connected to the network.

While it seems we 'go to' an Internet property (like a Web site), we may in fact be 'going to' lots of files dispersed all over the world. This is not a physical place.

People we communicate with can take on any guise they choose. Many activities encourage people to take on different personalities. I have several e-mail addresses and none of them is the same. You can never be sure who you may be exchanging information with and 'anyone can say or do anything' (not quite true but nearly true). We are in 'cyberspace'.

This virtual aspect of the Internet adds a lot of interest for practitioners who are using it for communication. There are some pretty obvious pitfalls, especially when campaigns involve aspects of opinion forming, attitude change and influences over behaviour. The last is very important because people using the Internet are interacting with its content. They are already in a behaviour changing 'frame of mind'.

E-mail

E-mail (electronic mail), the exchange of computer-stored messages, is the most used Internet facility; it is one of the earliest applications for the Internet and remains the most popular Net activity. E-mails can also be exchanged between and within private networks (such as intranets). E-mail can be distributed to lists of people as well as to individuals.

E-mail messages are usually encoded in ASCII (American Standard Code for Information Interchange) text, the most common format for text files in computers and on the Internet. E-mail is so flexible it can be used to transmit messages, URLs and non-text files, such as graphic and video images and sound files.

E-mail is one of the Internet protocols included with the TCP/IP suite of protocols. A popular protocol for sending e-mail is SMPT (Simple Mail Transfer Protocol) and a standard protocol for receiving it is via POP3 (Post Office Protocol 3). POP3 is a protocol in which e-mail is received and held for you on an Internet server (computer linked to the Internet). Periodically, you (or your client e-mail receiver) check your mailbox on the server and download any mail. IMAP (Internet Message Access Protocol) is a standard protocol for accessing e-mail from your server.

Mary Houten-Kemp provides a large resource of information and expertise at the Web site Everything e-mail: http://everythinge-mail.net.

Another comprehensive site about e-mail is provided by Heinz Tschabitscher at http://e-mail.miningco.com.

You can arrange to receive e-mail via the Web. This means you can download e-mails from anywhere including cybercafés as an alternative to setting up SMPT/POP3 links. For practitioners on the move, Web access to e-mail is very helpful because you do not need to take a laptop with you and only need access to an Internet connected computer to stay in touch – anywhere in the world.

The Web and Web sites

Lots of people think of the World Wide Web ('WWW' or 'the Web') as being the Internet. Sure, it's a very popular Internet protocol. It is supervised by the World Wide Web Consortium (http://www.w3.org/) and is based on the application of a set of writing conventions (Internet grammar) called Hypertext Transfer Protocol (HTTP).

Unlike so many of the inventions that have moved the world, this one truly was the work of one man... the World Wide Web is Berners-Lee's alone. He designed it. He loosed it on the world. And he more than anyone else has fought to keep it open, non-proprietary, and free... It's hard to overstate the impact of the global system he created. It's almost Gutenbergian. He took a powerful communications system that only the élite could use and turned it into a mass medium.

Time Magazine

A Web site is a related collection of Web (HTTP) files that includes a beginning file (page) called a home page. A company or an individual tells you how to get to their Web site by giving you the address of their home page. From the home page, you can get to all (or most of) the other pages on their site. HTTP is a language that many practitioners need to know and they also need to understand an adaptation of this language called NewsML, which is the online language of the news media. The International Press Telecommunications Council (IPTC) Guides are available from their site at http://www.iptc.org.

Internet protocols can be 'nested' in each other, which is a bit confusing. For example, e-mail and discussion lists can be 'nested' into Web pages. It is possible to 'nest' one Web site into another such as a virtual press office, or 'nest' a URL into an e-mail. The practitioner who can apply the power of Web sites and breadth of Internet protocols from a strong understanding of their capability has a significant communication advantage.

Newsgroups

A newsgroup is a discussion about a particular subject consisting of contributions written to one of a number of Internet properties and redistributed through Usenet, a network of computers using the Usenet protocols.

USENET NEWSGROUPS

A simple way of looking at Usenet newsgroups is to visit http://wwwdejanews.com. This service allows you to search newsgroups for messages matching your keywords. You can then reply or post your own message.

There are very big resources available for Usenet users. http://metalab.unc.edu/usenet-i/home.html is a Usenet information centre and good for people using Netscape. Information about Usenet is also available at http://www.faqs.org/usenet. *How Usenet Information Moves Round the Internet* by Jacob Palme, Department of Computer and Systems Sciences, Stockholm University, helps you understand how it works: http://www.dsv.su.se/~jpalme/e-mail-book/usenet-news.html.

There were over 2,000 contributions about UK supermarkets in December 2000 in 300 different newsgroups viewed by probably 9,000 people. In advertising terms, this represents 18 million 'opportunities to see' (OTS). Usenet is like a 'letters to the editor' column in cyberspace but without an editor. It is a worldwide (but virtual) network of online discussion groups.

Usenet uses a different protocol to the WWW and e-mail, called Network News Transfer Protocol. The technology to use NNTP is included as part of Netscape, Internet Explorer and other Web browser software and there are many other technologies available to access NNTP.

Internet mailing lists

A mailing list is a list of people who subscribe to a periodic mailing distribution on a particular topic. E-mail addresses are collected in a variety of ways, often because users elect to receive postings via e-mail. People elect to use such services because they trust the list manager to send relevant and only relevant information. Being on a mailing list is a popular way of keeping up with topics of interest or which are professionally significant. Many software producers and other vendors use them as a way to keep in touch with customers and customers use them to stay abreast of change.

MAILING LISTS

See http://www.liszt.com/which also has a good list of IRC chat sites.

A resource to find lists on any subject is at: http://catalog.com/vivian/interest-group-search.html. It is comprehensive but by no means complete. The popular PR mailing lists are very active and can be found at: http://groups.yahoo.com.

Sending e-mail messages from opt-in lists is a different form of publicity and is often closely associated with direct mail and spam. While this is a form of communication that the practitioner should know about, it is more of a marketing area than PR. One of the most important sites to help practitioners understand the rules and best practice for this area of publicity and marketing is the Direct Marketing Association at http://www.the-dma.org.

Instant messaging

Instant messaging (IM) lets you communicate with people over the Internet in real time. You can send and receive messages instantly because – unlike using e-mail – you don't have to wait for messages to download from a server. Because of this real-time interaction, instant messages are better for capturing subtle nuances in communication.

Instant messaging is similar to chat technology. However, chats usually take place within a Web browser plug-in (a little computer program or Java script), and instant messengers are stand-alone programs you download and install. Examples include Yahoo! Messenger, ICQ, and Microsoft's Instant Messenger. People who know each other, especially co-workers and business associates, who want to communicate in real time without any delays, typically use instant messages. A growing application for PR practitioners is to keep their IM program running and give out its address to journalists who can then make enquiries, 'converse' and check facts with the practitioner as they write their story.

INSTANT MESSAGING

Like chat programs, most instant messengers are available for free. ICQ (http://Web.icq.com/), MSN (http://msn.co.uk/), AIM (http://www.aol.com/aim/) and Yahoo! Messenger (http://messenger.yahoo.com/) are just a few of the messaging programs available.

Human Click allows you to attach an invitation to chat to online press releases (http://www.humanclick.com).

Bulletin boards

A BBS (bulletin board system) is a place where information can be put on display and accessed, with two computers linked directly to each other by modem. Thus one actually 'dials into' a bulletin board.

You can read information and can add information (if you have the relevant authority). Some bulletin boards are moderated. All of them are subject specific. Some are free and some are paid for services while others have restricted membership and a lot of them are private.

Bulletin board systems originated and generally operate independently of the Internet but a number also have Web sites and can be accessed via the WWW.

Members of the Institute of Public Relations have access to a bulletin board at the IPR's Web site, which is used as a discussion list.

BULLETIN BOARDS

BBSs have their own culture and jargon. For more information visit Boardwatch at: http://www.boardwatch.com. You can look at some commercial vendors here:

Inside The Web   www.insidetheWeb.com
Talk City   www.talkcity.com
The Globe   www.theglobe.com
Forum One   www.forumone.com
E-circle   http://www.ecircle-uk.com

Chat

On the Internet, chatting is talking to other people who are using the Internet at the same time as you. This is 'real-time' communication. Usually, this 'talking' is the exchange of typed-in messages requiring one site as the repository for the messages (or 'chat site') and a group of users who take part from anywhere on the Internet. With the advent of Internet voice channels, a lot of chat sites provide voice connection as well as the written word.

In some cases, a private chat can be arranged between two parties who meet initially in a group chat. Chats can be ongoing or scheduled for a particular time and duration; pop stars and footballers often 'chat' to fans like this.

Most chats are focused on a particular topic of interest and some involve guest experts or famous people who 'talk' to anyone joining the chat. Transcripts of a chat can be archived for later reference by chat room hosts, depending on the technologies used.

Chat is ephemeral and has some value in shaping ideas in a fast-moving environment. Applications by PR practitioners to engage constituents can bring very fast reaction, results and changes in attitudes. There are some chat rooms that have been known to influence share prices quite dramatically.

Jumping into a chat room without first seeing what is accepted and the language used is fraught with hazards. Lurk before you leap. Most people use nicknames in chat rooms and their real identity is hidden. Depending on the type of network, nicknames can be reserved (registered) or just used during the session. Some channels encourage users to register a nickname that is always used and even offer space for a personal profile, picture, and personal home page links. The BBC chat site is a good example of an organization offering chat as part of the richness of its site (http://www.bbc.co.uk/livechat).

CHAT

After downloading an IRC program and installing it, you type back and forth to each other on your computer screens. You can talk in groups or in private with only one person. Alternatively you can use a Java-enabled browser to visit a Web page with a chat room, and the chat window loads automatically. The three major IRC networks are: DALnet (http://www.dal.net/), Undernet (http://www.undernet.org/) and Efnet (http://www.efnet.org/). The Para Chat site is at: http://www.parachat.com.

For information about Chat technology see: http://www.newircusers.com/ircchat.html.

MUDs

A MUD is defined as a multi-user domain, multi-user dungeon, or multi-user dimension, all of which are referring to the same thing – an environment where multiple people may be logged on and interacting with one another, mostly to play games. Designed as a social experience on the Internet, it is managed by a computer program with a loosely organized context or theme (such as a rambling old castle with many rooms, or a period in national history). Some MUDs are ongoing adventure games; others are educational in purpose. There are MUD applications for a variety of commercial communications activities and they offer an interesting and exciting form of communication for PR practitioners.

Digital storytelling, when linked to a network, potentially changes the nature of the audience by inviting greater interaction with the storyteller (in effect, the audience members all become storytellers). Companies can tell their brand stories interactively, in ways that connect one-to-one to their customers and connect their customers with each other. Digital storytelling can be used in organizations to help individuals report back to the company about what they've learnt on business trips and at conferences.

MUDs existed prior to the World Wide Web, accessible through Telnet to a computer that hosted the MUD. MUDs are sometimes accessed through a Web site and some are perhaps better known as 3-D worlds or chat centres.

MUDS

Mudconnector is one of the more interesting MUD sites and is full of useful information; see http://www.mudconnector.com/index.html.

Telnet

Telnet is the way you can access someone else's computer (the host computer), assuming they have given you permission. The Web or (HTTP) protocol and the file transfer protocol (FTP) allow you to request specific files from remote computers, but not to actually be logged on as a user of that computer. With Telnet, you log on as a regular user with whatever privileges you may have been granted to the specific application and data on that computer. Then you can download a file such as text, a photograph or a computer program.

FTP is the simplest way to exchange files between computers on the Internet and is used to download and upload programs and other files to your computer from other servers and vice versa. These file transfer technologies are rapidly becoming the means by which special access and marketing advantage is achieved. FTP is a common way of distributing photographs and video.

The Internet is really a lot of technologies that can work together because they obey one of many protocols. The protocols are available to everyone and so anyone can use them. The practitioner needs to know about them and also needs expertise close to hand to be able to use and optimize the benefits.

WAP

WAP (Wireless Application Protocol) is a specification for a set of communication protocols to standardize the way that wireless devices, such as cellular telephones and radio transceivers, can be used for Internet access, including e-mail, the World Wide Web, newsgroups, and Internet relay chat. While Internet access has been possible in the past, different manufacturers have used different technologies. In the future, devices and service systems that use WAP will be able to interoperate.

Four companies conceived the WAP: Ericsson, Motorola, Nokia and Unwired Planet (which is now Phone.com). WAP and a related protocol (WASP) usher in a new range of communications tools, devices and challenges. Mobile phones are the first manifestation of these communications opportunities, but interactive PDAs (personal digital assistants) such as Hewlett-Packard's Palmtop and 3Com's PalmPilot followed on quickly and more are arriving by the day.

London taxi drivers may be one of the first to feel the impact of non-phone WAP. There is no need for 'The Knowledge' – knowing the whereabouts of every street and address – if such information can be relayed to the cab by WAP.

WAP SEARCH ENGINES

See:
http://mobile.alltheWeb.com; http://www.waply.com
http://somewherenear.com; http://mopilot.com
http://wapwarp.com/; http://wapaw.com/index.html

THE STUFF

Oh, so much to learn and so relevant to a communicator! Just as we learnt about using communications channels like brochures and employee newsletters, media relations with newspapers, radio and television, we now have to find out about these newer opportunities. So how are you going to learn all this stuff? There is the local night school and there are courses; these are the best ways to find out more in a structured way. It is worth ensuring that the course you aim for includes WWW, FTP, e-mail, Usenet, discussion lists, bulletin boards, instant messaging, MUDs and WAP.

The interesting thing is that the people at such courses come from all walks of life and every profession. This information is for everyone and knowing it does not confer any special advantage on the PR practitioner. This is commodity information. Anyone can do it even though it is a basic essential for the PR professional.

One of the best places to learn more is at home, in front of your own PC. This is a good place to practise too.

This may seem to represent a huge opportunity but, as we will see in the final chapter, there are even greater opportunities already waiting for you.

The public relations industry has, historically, sought a flexible way to create common information formats (such as press releases, backgrounders, in-house journals etc). This allowed people to use information in a convenient way. Now there is an exciting new way of achieving this on the Web. XML (Extensible Markup Language) is emerging, as this book goes to print, as a powerful new way that the publishing, business management and hundreds of other management processes can use common information formats. Using XML, we can share both the format and the data on the World Wide Web, intranets, and elsewhere. For example, PR practitioners are beginning to agree on a standard or common way to describe information in press releases (headings, copy, contact details, photographs and so forth) and then describe the press release format with XML. Such a standard way of describing data will enable a user (eg newspaper, magazine, television station) to send an intelligent computer agent (a program) to each practitioner's Web site, gather data, and then make decisions about inclusion in a news story for a PC, WAP phone, PDA, public kiosk and other Internet communications channels. XML can be used by any individual or group of individuals or companies that wants to share information in a consistent way.

In due course, and this is months not years away, XML will be very important to practitioners and there will be a need for more comprehensive detail to be available to the public relations sector.

3

Being respected in cyberspace

For a student of social order, what needs to be explained is not the amount of conflict but the great amount of sharing and cooperation that does occur in online communities.[1]

Approaching others in cyberspace can be refreshingly direct or can be a cautious affair. When participants are considering exchanges of information and products for money, a range of factors comes into play. Up front or shy, the actors size each other up to see if they are good partners for desirable interaction. The evidence that the trusting relationship is not all that it seems comes from many quarters.

WHY TRUST IS SO IMPORTANT

At the Third Biennial Conference on the Internet and Society, Professor Kollock, whose studies of online communities go back

---

[1] Kollock, P (1999) The economies of online cooperation: gifts and public goods in cyberspace, in eds Mark Smith and Peter Kollock, *Communities in Cyberspace*, Routledge, London

the early 1990s, invoked the need to create communities that embrace the architecture of, among other things, trust. 'We need an architecture of reputation,' he added. 'An architecture of accountability.'

Kollock puts the relationships between free exchanges of information (including especially Internet exchanges) into a commercial perspective:

> For the person deciding whether to enter into a transaction, the partner's reputation is a source of information that can reduce uncertainty and guide the decision of whether to trust the partner. Because of this same dynamic, the existence of shared reputations serves as an incentive for the partner to be trustworthy because of the damaging effects of acquiring a bad reputation. However, the threatened or actual sanction of acquiring a bad reputation will only be effective to the extent that accurate information is collected and disseminated among likely exchange partners. If people do not talk among themselves, if the information exchanged is inaccurate, or if a person can hide their identity, then reputation systems will not be an effective means of managing risk.

Whinston and Zhang examined the significance of trust and its relationship with security technologies (see the box below). They say that there is a balance between security of transmitted information and the trusted reputation of an organization, which interplay to build effective relationships. 'Some of the major obstacles for electronic commerce include security, quality and uncertainty,' they say.

In her article 'If you build it, will they come', reporting the Third Biennial Conference on the Internet and Society, Laura Lambert reports Professor Peter Kollock proposing 'an architecture of reputation'. Published in harvard.net.news: http://www.hno. harvard.edu/net_news2000/06.02.WEB/design.html

In 'The production of trust in online markets', *Advances in Group Processes*, Vol. 16, JAI Press, Kollock goes further into risk and reputation.

A B Whinston and H Zhang look at the impact of technology on reputation in 'The impact of authentication and reputation on competition in the electronic markets', in M Fehimovic (ed), *Electronic Commerce in Europe*, World Markets Research Centre, London, 1999.

The concept of trust is well expressed by Alison Clark in an unpublished paper she prepared for the Joint Institute of Public Relations and Public Relations Consultants' Association PR Internet Commission (see Figure 3.1). These values, and often associated corporate and brand identity, have to be zealously guarded in the Internet era and have to be a component part of corporate culture if they are to survive the influences of added Internet porosity and added transparency.

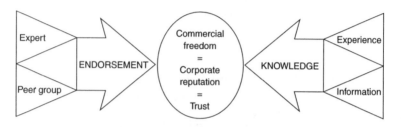

Figure 3.1   *The Clark 'Trust' diagram*

The Internet is a massive resource for expertise, and online relationships form a powerful peer group. For these reasons the Internet has become a very effective arena for the development of endorsement. Few organizations can ignore this potential, especially as it can be powerful as both a positive and negative influence.

THE PR INTERNET COMMISSION

In the summer of 1999, a working group of people, drawn from the Institute of Public Relations and the Public Relations Consultants' Association, was formed to examine the influence of the Internet on the practice of PR. Twelve papers were submitted with a number of associated supplements produced in the following months. The papers can be viewed at: http://www.geocities.com/dphillips4363/IPR_PRCA_Commission.html.

When the power of the Internet is used to build trust, reputation is enhanced and organizations are able to build powerful relationships. Trusted partners are much more likely to be able to do new things such as change prices, add services, streamline operations, etc. This means that with a trusted reputation, they are freer to compete.

Through trust, we build reputation and commercial freedom. Trust has to be pervasive throughout an organization before it can be manifest online because, in every instance, reputation management will, to greater or lesser degree, take cognisance of how an organization is perceived in cyberspace.

This is an area for the practitioner to be concerned with in an Internet world. It requires continuous monitoring and 'tasting' for porosity and what the wired world (including the posted information which has been transformed by Internet agency — see below) is saying about the company and its related products, services and issues. Anything that reduces the level of trust between an organization and its constituency is bad news and requires immediate remedial attention.

Inevitably, every company will be managed on the basis of the issues its directors face.

Trustworthy

Planning and implementation of strategies and actions to resolve online (and offline) issues (be they benign or threatening) are only valid when the effect on existing or latent publics has been thoroughly explored.

Today, it is unethical for a practitioner to promote a site that does not conform to these basic principles. This is especially true if the practitioner does not specifically advise the client or organization on the need for adequate security and capacity of their Internet implementation and back office support.

If the site a PR practitioner promotes goes down because the level of publicity drives too much traffic to the site for the organization to cope, then the site owner is culpable. However, if the practitioner has not properly and robustly advised the site owner of this potential risk to reputation he or she has an even greater responsibility and is negligent of the client's reputation.

The practitioner should research the client and the client's product. This is a fundamental for all PR practice.

Advising organizations on issues of security

A major UK clearing bank unsettled consumer confidence in online banking service with three mishaps in August 2000. It's experience offers practitioners lessons about online reputation.

First, its system allowed users into other people's bank accounts. Second, a user accidentally stumbled across his next-door neighbour's finances. Third, its online offering failed a security check when customers logged out of their accounts and then clicked the back button on their browser to find themselves still logged in. The media gave the incidents a full hearing and the criticism in newsgroups was rapid and continued for several weeks.

This ineptitude reflected badly on the bank and the banking industry's reputation for being able to offer online services. As this was the second online bank in seven months to publicly demonstrate such failures, it also appeared that UK bankers are not prepared to learn lessons. This delayed the availability of online banking for months, giving competitors (notably from France) an excellent opportunity to gain markets and market share.

The PR professional can learn from experiences to date and advise clients on the impact on reputation of breaches in security and compromised e-commerce programmes. It is the duty of the PR professional to invest in the related issues and crisis management capability for when such accidents occur.

THE REPUTATION OF ONLINE STOCKBROKING

A number of stockbrokers implemented Web sites to allow people to trade shares online. They promoted their services with great panache using above and below the line advertising and as well as PR consultants. The campaigns were very successful. The brokers were overwhelmed by the response and, when the market was very active, discovered that they could not cope with all the trades requested by their online clients. There were questions in parliament and the regulator threatened to close down the services. The reputation of the companies for online share dealing was seriously damaged, and market leadership in Europe in January 2000 had evaporated by the following August.

The practitioners who promoted these companies to the extent that they were overwhelmed were actively engaged in the ultimate humiliation of their clients. The reputation of their clients and the relationship between their clients and a number of important stakeholders was damaged by the naive actions of the publicity practitioners involved.

There is the case of a public utility, Powergen. Its online service compromised the credit card details of its customers by listing them on a publicly available Web page. Ten days after it had been informed of this security issue, it made the following statements to the BBC: 'We take the security of customers' personal information very seriously' and, 'We are urgently considering what we need to do to inform customers whose records have been accessed, and we have provided information to the police who are investigating.' To sign up for the online service, its customers have to provide their e-mail address.

The question in the mind of the consumer whose personal information was left exposed to several hundred million Internet users for 10 days can only be guessed at. The quality of the ethics of a company that believes this approach can be regarded as 'taking the security of customers' personal information seriously' may be questioned. In the meantime the quality of management that cannot inform 7,000 people that their credit card details are known to several third parties, the police, a magazine and the world at large for 10 days is sloppy by most commercial standards. The Internet community is perfectly capable of asking if the company is as cavalier with its shareholders' information. The shareholders still support the company, which may reflect on those institutions as well! Or to put it into the language of the Internet: 'Would you trust your pension to the fund that invests in Powergen?'

But the responsibilities do not rest there. There are ethical dilemmas that need to be thought through.

Ethical dilemmas

In France it is illegal to exhibit or sell objects with racist overtones, including Nazi memorabilia. Yahoo!, a global provider of information about everything, includes information to enable surfers to access the aforesaid memorabilia. This is done through a number of its wholesale and retail outlets (Yahoo.com, Yahoo.co.uk, etc). It was alleged that Yahoo! was breaking French law by hosting an auction site that sells Neo-Nazi, Nazi and Ku Klux Klan objects.

Yahoo! said it was against the American constitution to make the US-based operations comply with the resulting court order. Yahoo! did not want to break the law in France and so did not offer its full information service in France and blocked access from its French site to the auction. However, there is nothing to stop a Frenchman going to the Canadian version of Yahoo! to find out about any Internet content. For the Americans the issue is this. No one is forcing a consumer to visit these sites but everyone should have the right to visit if they so choose, however contemptible. Yahoo! was threatened with a national boycott in France (at a time when it was under threat from its leading Internet presence by the French portal, Wanadoo).

Yahoo! has a domestic dilemma because of the US constitutional issues (the First Amendment). Internationally, the US constitution and freedom of information are only a paper-thin concept, as Yahoo! proved on 11 August when its news site showed the Reuters report:

Yahoo! faces Nazi site verdict

A French judge is due to rule on whether the US Internet company, Yahoo!, should comply with the law in France and prevent French Internet users from one of its Web sites. The site sells Nazi memorabilia which, under French law is considered to be material that incites racism. 11 August, 9:47 am GMT

But on 11 August, Yahoo! denied access to the full Reuters story from its server, thus compromising its position as an unbiased news retailer.

While this is a case of the biter bit, it throws up a host of ethical issues. The significance of this event is not that it is important in terms of the Internet, rather that it requires practitioners to think through the ethics of their organizations and their approach to business.

On the one hand there is the guidance of the law. This is fine, except, of course, the Internet is global and the law is not necessarily the same from nation to nation. There is the guidance of public opinion, but that is often fickle and subject to wild outbursts and unreasoned, if temporary, passion.

When faced with issues of ethics, the practitioner will always defer to the high ground and will thereby be able to sustain a consistent approach. Any other course, with the resulting and inevitable ducking, weaving, spin and half-truths, will come to haunt the organization for a long time both online and offline.

The historic role for PR as advocate and bridge between organization and the public has a long way to go in the age of the Internet.

THE NEW SKILLS

PR practitioners now work in an international industry. Their work is of a global nature. The simple process of an article published because of a PR initiative, or a White Paper published on the company Web site suddenly pitches the practitioner on to a global stage. This exciting and exhilarating idea, where we talk to different peoples and interact with a range of cultures, transforms PR at a stroke.

The Internet has, additionally, brought relationships and reputation to the fore. This is as true for the practitioner as for organizations, and the consequence is that best practice has to prevail. The organization is now closer to its stakeholders than ever before. It touches them directly. An e-mail to a chief executive opens up opportunities for interrelationships that were once slow and now are fast and intimate. The content of the Web site and comment in newsgroups offers kinship between individuals and the community interested in your organization that was not possible before.

Where there was spin, there must be transparency and where there was publicity there has to be empathy. Presentation, accessibility and transparency with opinion formers and journalists are essential for future media relations. Effective use of e-mail, the Web and other Internet resources is now becoming a necessity. Creating relationships with online information partners, ambassadors and management of issues-driven third parties is a necessary skill.

The practitioner needs to be able to surf, create libraries of reliable online resources, and interact with online properties and their most significant contacts. Well-executed research puts the PR practitioner at the centre of knowledge acquisition. Because content derived from internal resources, information partners and wider Web sources can be intelligently made available by the practitioner, the practice of PR becomes, de facto, the core and essential knowledge centre in the organization. As a trusted repository of leading knowledge gleaned from internal and external resources, the practitioner moves to the centre of competitive advantage.

Issues and issues management, far from being an area of practice when things go wrong, now also enhances opportunities when things are going right.

THE NEW ROLE FOR PR

Driven by what we know of global transparency and community as it affects organizations, the practitioner has to elevate the practice of public relations not merely into the boardroom but into the very heart of management. The PR industry will need to be robust in pointing out the need for enterprise-wide protection of reputation based on ethical practice.

Practitioners now need to indulge in a great deal of high-quality thinking and have to stand back from the hurly-burly of daily activity to examine the implications of e-enablement, e-business and e-commerce but more especially e-relationships and reputation. This is becoming part of everyday life and has to bring with it the influences and activities of day-to-day offline living.

The idea that one may 'add' an Internet element to PR fails to grasp its significance. It enables, enhances and invigorates communication, relationships and reputation and as such is the means by which older forms of PR practice and process can be transformed. Cyberspace is not a place for practitioners to retreat into; rather it is an extension of what we have always done — facilitate the very best of relationships in the full glare of transparency before a global public.

The dynamic of the Internet requires the practitioner to be proactive. Not implementing Internet strategies and processes will harm the potential of the organization. A journalist who cannot make contact, a recommended Web resource that is not reliable, inappropriate use of communications delivery platforms and channels, are all areas that require action sooner rather than later.

Our organizations and clients will need practitioners who have the widest understanding of PR and the processes, products and services offered to stakeholders. They will need our best endeavours in processing information and managing knowledge.

Combined with creative ideas, new and old skills, the global stage is now available and there is nothing to stop PR practitioners from being at its centre.

THE ROLE OF THE INSTITUTIONS

The PR institutions have a significant role to play in helping and advising their members. The ability to offer services to clients and the changed ethical and best practice issues are quite significant.

THE PR INSTITUTIONS ALERTS

The government's Performance and Innovation Unit (PIU) report in 1999 (ecommerce@its.best) promoted three pillars for the future success of e-commerce. They were: understanding, trust and access. The Institute of Public Relations and the Public Relations Consultants' Association received notice of these issues on 27 October 1999 from the PR Internet Commission in its response to the government report.

The PR Internet Commission recommendations specifically say:

- para 49. That best practice teaching and knowledge transfer for practitioners shall address trust issues;
- para 50. That the industry working party shall examine trust issues closely and work with other sectors in establishing both best practice and (policed) professional codes of conduct;
- para 51. That the industry prepares clear guidelines for practitioners in matters of security and trust;
- para 52. That the industry identifies the issues of security to practitioners;
- para 53. That the industry becomes both associated with and active in the implementation of secure e-commerce.

The practitioner not advising on consequential damage to relationships and reputation as well as seeking adequate and comprehensive assurances about sufficient security, is negligent in the practice of PR. The practitioner bears a responsibility 'to conduct his or her professional activities with proper regard to the public interest' (Clause 2 of the IPR Code of Professional Conduct) and practitioners should be aware of examples of lost reputation in similar circumstances evidenced throughout the media. There is a silver lining to this apparent cloud. It puts the practice of ethical public relations at the core of management.

The chapters that follow offer you ideas and practical applications for transition from the old economy into the post-network era.

4

Integrating communication

Web sites, extranets, intranets and e-mail provide ready means for communication. In some organizations they are an integrated set of technologies. In others they are very separate and integrate in a rather chaotic way.

Intranets are closed and are only (for the most part) available to, typically, employees. Extranets are a process whereby internal information (from intranets and/or the organization's databases and e-mail) interacts with chosen information or commercial partners. This information is typically meant to be confidential between the two parties, the organization and selected stakeholders. Web sites are predominantly open and visible to anyone.

By using the combination of facilities available from intranets, extranets and Web sites, organizations can obtain far-reaching communication advantages. For companies, such advantages can bring dramatic reductions in costs, add to customer benefits and increase competitive advantages that far outstrip any other form of investment.

Shel Holtz points up the differences between the old and the new economies.[1] They have significant implications for the PR practitioner:

Industrial Economy	*Information Economy*
Top down	Networked
Based on quantity	Based on quality
Batch processed	Customized
Producer driven	Customer driven

His analysis translates easily into what we know today. We can already draw PR analogies.

We are moving from command and control structures to informed and connected networks of internal and external constituents. PR once addressed commanders and controllers (of information) and now has to engage constituents.

The industrial economy benefited from volume. The PR industry sought column inches in the high-circulating publications. Today, people will not pay for heavily discounted but inferior mass-produced product but will pay a premium for bespoke quality. The PR industry has to offer tangible benefits through individual briefing and rich content to meet the expectations of relevant constituents and achieve optimum and measurable changes in opinion, attitude or behaviour.

Where the industrial economy wanted economies of scale and exactly the same product in high volumes, today's consumers demand options, choice and individual attention. In PR, journalists look for the unique angle and the constituents 'pull' specific and wanted information as and when they need it. The day of mass press release mailing, spammed e-mail and employee newspapers has given way to individual, personalized and available interaction.

Before, it was the producer who filled the markets with goods but today it is the customer who demands satisfaction. How can we make all this happen?

[1] Holtz, S (1999) *Public Relations on the Net Amacon*, American Management Associations, New York

INTEGRATING WEB SITES, EXTRANET AND INTRANETS

The Internet enablement structure for many organizations can provide a seamless and common relationship between external constituents (Web site and completely transparent information), partners (extranet transparency that is shared with selected external partners) and internal stakeholders (transparency that is only available to people and processes within the organization). This integrated process enhances navigation for internal and partner organizations. It is also the means for information osmosis from internal to external audiences providing capability by which transparency can be managed.

Diagrammatically the integration of intranet, extranet and Web presence could (idealistically) look like Figure 4.1. This kind of structure allows protective barriers to be installed (called firewalls), which prevent confidential information from being exposed.

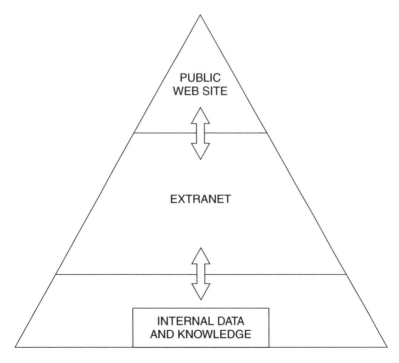

Figure 4.1 *Flow of transparency*

You can now see how all activities and information point towards the customer and consumer (Web) public, which is different to old hierarchies where the organization chart had the CEO at the top and the customer positioned below the salesman at the bottom.

The interdepartmental flow of information

The problem associated with providing an information structure is that it must be understandable, and navigation to information has to be simple for everybody. It needs to be a form or landscape that the human mind can comprehend. The capability of computing makes it easy to create a landscape that is complex and looks like spaghetti to the user.

The secret for managers and communication advisers is to create simple standardized access for people throughout organizations. One way of making information accessible in an understandable form is by offering knowledge 'streams'. Such streams can (actually or apparently) flow through from internal (intranet) to external (Web) audiences and can be accessible between people with cross-departmental (knowledge) interests.

Streaming knowledge in a corporate environment may mean that streams could be about management, financial information, product management, marketing and sales, people management or the processes attached to external constituents. Alternatively, streams can be subject based. In addition, an organization can have both/all types of structure. This is not an either/or choice but a mixture to suit the needs of the organization's constituents.

In modern organizations, streams of information and knowledge can readily interact and bring really big advantages. In his book, *Business@the Speed of Thought*, Microsoft's founder Bill Gates shows how this works in practice for organizations of all sizes, including Microsoft. Such streaming structures may look like Figure 4.2. In such a structure, finding information in any stream is only a few clicks of a mouse away and interdepartmental exchanges are facilitated.

This kind of approach also allows for information to be protected by firewalls between different streams of knowledge such as between purchase prices from suppliers to retail prices to a customer. In the Internet-enabled organization, it is easy to create a new stream.

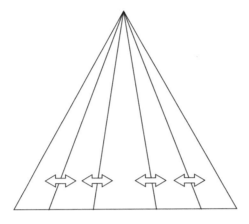

Figure 4.2 *Knowledge streams*

Knowledge access models

The combination of hierarchical and interdisciplinary structures (management processes/streamed knowledge) with managed transparency for both internal and external access is very advantageous. By combining the streamed knowledge and access models, an integrated approach is possible and is an aid to development of e-enablement strategies. Using such models, organizations can develop e-enablement activities with a very quick return on investment. This is a case of communications strategies adding high returns for every form of organization and every application of e-enablement.

With an enterprise-wide commonality of structure the culture of an organization has the means to find expression and corporate brand equity evident to all.

Within this organization it is easy for cells of interest to form between departments and without hierarchies. The important nucleus is the person or group that can identify an issue and recruit solutions from any part of the organization or beyond.

The concept that allows administrative information and an organization's knowledge to be transparently available means that knowledge can move through an organization easily. It also makes organizations more porous. By identifying the boundaries for transmission of knowledge, organizations can keep confidential information from external audiences. Most companies use firewalls in their local networks and intranets. As a general rule, being

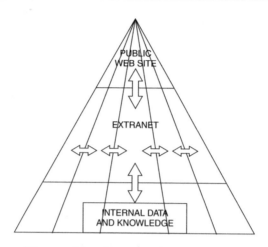

Figure 4.3   *Integrated transparency*

able to identify confidential information while making as much other information and knowledge generally available as possible is the best approach.

Not only will information be available at any point in the new organic 'organization' chart, but also the content may be accessed at any point. Thus the 100-page briefing document may be accessed for the first time at page 47 and the careful contexting statements in the first paragraph are missed. This changes how we prepare information and how constituents will understand it. A simple experiment is to access (as the BBC invites us to do) www.bbc.co.uk and then access www.bbc.co.uk./today. The information is from the same organization but the impression of the organization is completely different. This means that you need to put yourself in the mind of the networked constituent when building a site, or writing for an online consumption.

The management of (information/knowledge) transparency will reflect the style of an organization. It will require continuous reassessment and organic transformation. In addition, the means for transparency through the use of other delivery channels, including fixed communication systems such as Electronic Data Interchange (EDI) and Web-enabled technologies such as WAP, will be a process that can evolve all the time.

These processes do look very formal and mechanistic. In fact, they offer opportunities for interdepartment, multiple skill groups to form with a minimum of obstruction and bureaucracy. They can and should be applied with passion and incorporated with a sense of the fun and in the spirit of the Internet (but without compromising security or causing time delays which, in the end, are just frustrating).

Organizations with a Web culture typically make access to extranet and intranet information available to employees via their public Web site home page. In this way the public Internet presence, navigation and the corporate persona, are seen by all every day. Employees entering organizational intranets via some other virtual route will note that they have been relegated to the virtual staff entrance or via a virtual bicycle shed. The typical manifestation of such an approach is the telephone receptionist who can't tell an enquirer the organization's URL!

This form of corporate re-engineering will fail when organizations attempt to 'stitch' the Internet into existing and unchanged corporate hierarchies. The result tends to look like a plumber's nightmare to the user and is usually hedged around with a mass of frustrating firewalls to prevent people finding information that they may well need to be more effective in their job.

The new reality already exists. Interdepartmental e-mail has already broken down many of the departmental barriers. Indeed, inter-company and inter-institution relationships have changed because of this ease of interdepartmental and inter-company communication. At the same time, senior managers and junior employees are now in direct contact in the same way. The gatekeeper can (and in some places does) e-mail the chief executive. Top to bottom communication is now a fact of life.

Using an extranet/Web structure to try to reimpose old hierarchies and fiefdoms will fail and will continue to fail. On the other hand, the ability to recast corporate structures through knowledge streams, which are organic by nature, is a powerful opportunity to lever up knowledge assets and rid organizations of costs and barriers to development, change and profitability.

PR practitioners, most notably those with internal communications roles, are now involved in the concepts and structures behind intranets. Thinking through the evolution of these systems as they interact with extranets and Web sites is the next and inevitable step. Internal communication is changing and will never again respond to old systems like cascaded message dissemination or management newsletters and notice boards without electronic integration. Neither can internal communication be divorced from external influences with information partners or publicly available competitors' information or consumer criticism.

The advent of the Internet and its new, internal, applications inevitably extends the role and responsibility of PR practice. Suddenly, either by design or default, organizations have become transparent. The role of the practitioner is to aid in the design and to plan for default, because of the inherent dangers to reputation and relationships as fiefdoms and organization's historic information gatekeepers become irrelevant.

E-enablement and the effect on reputation

The term 'e-enablement' has become common currency but understanding what it is and its resulting implications is not easy. It is important both for the practice of PR and for application to the management of PR departments and consultancies.

Almost every process in e-enablement involves communication within and outside organizations, the implication being that this interaction is relevant to communications professionals and not least PR practitioners. The seven parts of e-enablement are:

1. Awareness.
2. Motivation.
3. Rewards.
4. Involvement.
5. Contribution.
6. Sharing.
7. Cost benefit.

A practical example may help in understanding these processes.

In the past, practitioners spent a considerable amount of time identifying opinion formers' publications and journalists relevant to a story or campaign. Information was then sent to these outlets or was 'placed' as stories and variants on stories. The level of e-enablement was low but the means for creating awareness had been established.

Today, for e-enablement to succeed, the press release needs to motivate the journalist to seek more information by, for example, a visit to the virtual press office. That visit needs to be so rewarding that the journalist becomes involved. The virtual press office will provide a wide range of quickly accessible added information components designed to provide rich content for a stunningly good and highly contexted and newsworthy story, a rich reward for little effort.

The level of reward will be such that the journalist is prepared to make a contribution like offering information such as a name, address, publications details, etc, which, in turn, will add to future rewards. As this book goes to bed, rumours of self-creating, interactive and bespoke mutual news exchanges are coming to light.

The information provided by the journalist needs to be shared to be effective. For example, it can be automatically shared via the intranet with the advertising department to create a context-relevant advertising campaign. It may be shared with the Webmaster to seek links to the journalist/publication site or it may be to the librarian seeking information sources. These internal stakeholders will be able to access such information as and when required. They can combine it with other resources and create new and reliable knowledge and processes. It is a resource that is available but not intrusive.

The information will certainly enhance the practitioner's media targeting. Above all, the information provided will be volunteered and will have low cost of acquisition, maintenance and distribution. The return on investment is very high.

The PR practitioner will have cut out the cost of rebuilding the next press list and many people and departments have benefited from not much more than the collection of an e-mail address, the publication's URL and its circulation/site hit rate.

HELPFUL RULES TO KEEP BUDGETS SWEET

1. As far as you can, allow people to provide information because it is in their interest to do so.
2. Avoid making people collect or collate data unless it is in their interest to do so.
3. Automate.
4. Avoid systems that require information to be entered more than once.
5. Ensure there is a means of verification and an audit trail for the whole process.
6. Provide for revision, maintenance and redundancy (duplication in case of system breakdown).

Using these same processes, internal and external stakeholders can e-enable most corporate activities. Whether in procurement, sales and marketing, design and development or internal management systems the benefits follow.

More than a few PR practitioners have spurned involvement in the processes of e-enablement and business-to-business online relationship building. It will come back to haunt those who dismissed such extensive communication as being exclusive to the domains of the IT, sales or purchasing, perhaps finance and legal departments. From what has gone before in this book, it is evident that inappropriate relationships, messages and channels can quickly damage reputations and organizations' ability to succeed.

There is another aspect to e-enablement of concern to the practitioner. The nature of the relationship has to be responsive.

MANAGING ONLINE INFORMATION PARTNERS

The day BT declared 3,000 people redundant in 2000, its online recruitment partner, Monster.co.uk, advertised 1000 jobs online. The range of mixed messages generated by these two organizations is easy to see.

In the past, a human resources department would have pulled newspaper advertisements and no one would have noticed. Even if the advertisements continued, the effective reach of mixed messages would be negligible. Online, the potential audience, as well as the range of interested parties, is far greater and wider and, in this case, the evidence was observable for two weeks, which is a much longer life than for traditional print advertising. This case shows how a PR department has to be aware, and able to empower managers to think about corporate reputation both in terms of relations with their vendors and online (and offline) constituents.

This chapter shows how communications has become more integrated and affects internal and external publics and their relationship, one with another. It proposes that organizations restructure and re-engineer and that PR should take the leading role. The bald truth is that as more employees get e-mail, this restructuring is already in process. As employees thereby acquire more information (whether from the intranet, LAN or Internet) and knowledge jumps unnecessary firewalls (as it does), the changes outlined above are already well under-way.

In many cases the machine in the factory or warehouse is connected to the customer through a range of technologies. In many cases the person operating the machine is not connected at all. For the sake of the customer it may be helpful for the operator to be at least as well informed as the machine, especially when the machine makes a human-like mistake. Closer to home, the PR person may offer a story to a journalist but the Web server may be already automatically conducting a dialogue through the Web site. Under both circumstances, it becomes obvious why employees overcome management restrictions and bureaucratic obstruction to become participants. In other words, when people are frustrated they tend to 'cheat' the system.

You, the communications specialist, have the opportunity to facilitate, enhance and speed up the process of networked working, or at worst, to participate so as not to be completely over-taken by events.

5

Message transfer in cyberspace

In 2000, with 37 per cent of users surfing at work and 63 per cent surfing at home, the reach of the Internet was obviously a very personal thing and yet a significant part of the way people find out information as part of their occupation. This means that organizations are under the microscope from many directions. The highest proportion of Internet use is interactive with e-mail, instant messaging, chat, reading news and interactive activities (including shopping) high among the list of things people say they do. So, with millions of messages swirling around the Internet, it is important for the communications professional to understand what happens to these interactions.

There are three phenomena that are very important to the practice of PR: porosity, transparency and agency. They were identified and brought together by Anne Gregory for the Public Relations Internet Commission.

POROSITY

'Porosity' is the passage of information from within an organization to external audiences, outside the controlled and formal information flows, and without regard for the broader consequences of the communication.

Example

Attaching a tender document to an e-mail to amplify a technical point, and not realizing that this reveals the company's intent to redevelop the premises.

POROSITY CASE STUDIES

We know from experience that a lot of information 'leaks' from organizations. This company has, for its own reasons, collected a wide range of case studies: http://www.elronsoftware.com/press-room/casestudies.shtml#d.

TRANSPARENCY

'Transparency' is a deliberate opening of internal systems to people outside the organization, so that they have access to the same quality of data and information. Transparency need not be total – some areas of data remain closed – and may not be universal to all audiences.

Example

A courier company permits access to parcel tracking systems to those who have the consignment details.

AGENCY

'Agency' is the process of transformation of a message as it is passed from one person to another, and acts through the application to the original data of new context and understanding (including visual images) (see Figure 5.1). Agency is of itself neither benign nor malicious.

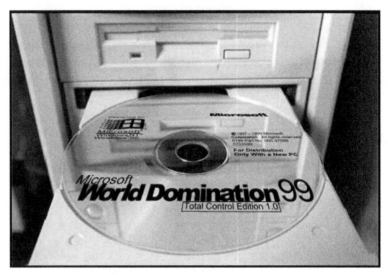

Figure 5.1   *Internet agency*

Source: taken from the Web at www.microsoft.sux.com

Throughout time organizations have been subject to transparency, porosity and agency as information flowed to their many stakeholders. The immediacy, network structure, global and pervasive nature of the Internet adds significantly to their potency.

A further contribution by Alison Clark bears close scrutiny.[1] Her analysis of the way messages move in the Internet is very instructive (see Figure 5.2).

The nature of communication using the Internet is an extension of current communications practice. The way information finds its way between people on the Internet requires some thought and the PR Internet Commission produced this view of how messages reach audiences.

The forms of communication are described in terms of one-to-many, targeted messages, Web messages that reach everyone and the nature of the network of networks. These processes mean messages can move round the Internet among a wide range of stakeholders very quickly.

There is a difference between traditional forms of communication and the new Internet-driven communication. The most notable changes are:

---

[1] Clark, A (1999) e-PR, paper presented to the Institute of Public Relations and Public Relations Consultant's Association Internet Commission

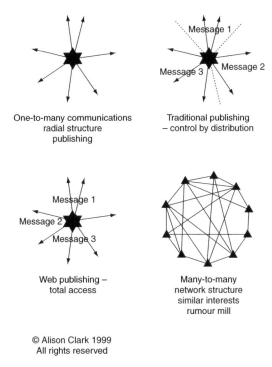

Figure 5.2 *Messages delivered to the Internet*

- the ability to communicate to large numbers of people and organizations;
- the speed by which such information can pass round the world;
- the extent to which information is and can be made available at the time, place and in the form that it is needed;
- the wide range of constituents who have access to information;
- the extent to which people and machines can and do change the nature of messages and re-release these morphed messages to the world.

The movement of information from an individual into a community offers networking capabilities that are enhanced by the Internet because its communications capabilities are very good. Examples of communications channels offering effective communications include e-mail, Usenet and newsgroups, chat, instant messaging and cookies.

The ability for information to circulate in a network of family, friends, colleagues and acquaintances is very effective when the

Internet is involved. It also makes it difficult for anyone to be the gatekeeper for organizational knowledge and it frequently means information 'leaks' out of organizations as well. 'Leaking' information (called porosity) is one of the most significant evolutionary changes for communication driven by the Internet. Information always leaked from organizations but today it reaches further, faster and from many more people and machines. In addition it is easily linked to other information for added potency.

The significance of the Internet is that it provides an easy capability for information to 'jump' from one network to another... and then to another and so on. For example, a story can circulate in newsgroups and then 'jump' to online news media and 'jump' again to broadcast media and then 'jump' again to Parliament and all the time still be followed in the newsgroups (see Figure 5.3).

This 'network of networks' is a very powerful part of Internet dynamics. It also means that a message will often change and morph in the retelling.

Information and messages that can (and almost always will eventually) reach into the Internet communication network, will rapidly become available to all stakeholders. An example may be a

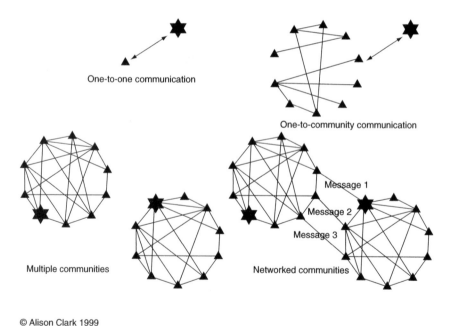

One-to-one communication

One-to-community communication

Multiple communities

Message 1
Message 2
Message 3

Networked communities

Figure 5.3   *How messages progress*

press release posted on a Web site. In the past, press releases were largely only available to journalists. Once posted to a Web site they are available to the news media, competitors, employees and consumers as well as a wider constituency. In addition, a press release issued to an online media distribution company has the same transparency. In principle the same can be said of product information, financial information and so forth.

Because information is posted by you (and by a lot of other people) it is available for anyone to see. You are no longer targeting messages. The nature of the organization is available for anyone to examine from the information made available by you and anyone else who wants to contribute via the Web site, e-mail or a chat room or even as a third party vendor, customer or employee. You have little control over either the message or the target. Life in PR has changed quite dramatically (see Figure 5.4).

There are many ways of visualizing how messages transfer in cyberspace and because it is an integrated process both inside and

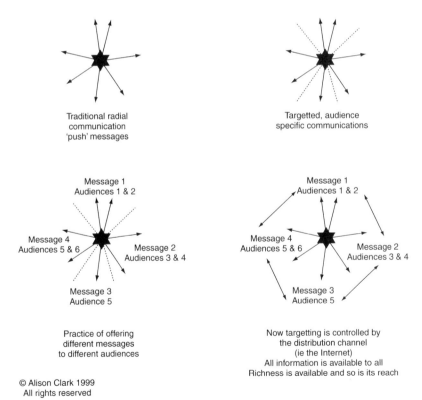

Figure 5.4 *Targeting is controlled by the network*

outside an organization, it is important to put it in perspective (see Figure 5.5).

Our job now is to facilitate mutual understanding for internal and external constituents. One of the most important constituents that will need help is the management team.

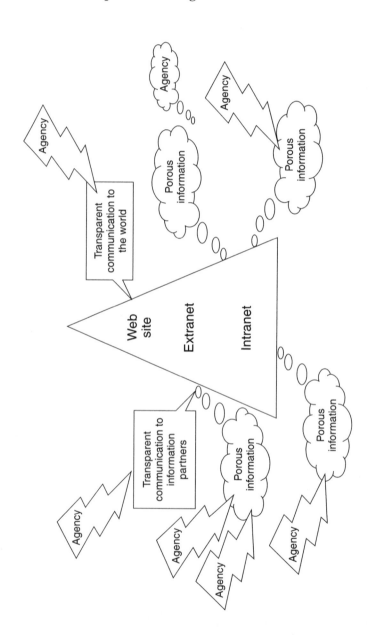

Figure 5.5 *The way messages move*

6

Surfing

No professional communicator can be effective unless he or she surfs. PR people need access to Internet information and knowledge. This means that practitioners need to become ace surfers. More realistically, you should be at least as good as most competent Internet users. To have access to the deeper recesses of the Internet you need specialist tools and expertise.

Using search facilities is easy, but to be very good at it requires some knowledge and lots of practice. The rewards can be very high and will save time and add to the richness of the PR offering for the whole organization. The PR practitioner who is not good at using the Internet as a research resource is at an immense disadvantage. The Internet is, among many things, a news medium in its own right. It is also the means by which a very high proportion of online and offline news is distributed. Practitioners need skills to find where all this is happening.

Surfing to find out about an organization, its vendors and customers, online and offline partners is easy and a great advantage. The extent to which its stories and news are current and competitive is evident from the Internet as are histories of its key employees and knowledge of its many other constituents. However, it is very easy to become 'lost in cyberspace', so there are some essentials that you need to know.

WHAT YOU ARE REALLY FINDING

When searching the Internet you may know the site you want to visit, for example http://www.homepagename.co.uk. By putting this in the address bar of your browser and clicking on 'go', you will go direct to the site you have selected. Alternatively you may click on an automatic link (http://www.homepagename.co.uk.) embedded in a Web page, e-mail or IM message, which your computer programme will automatically open.

The third way to find a Web site or a Web page is by using a search engine. Search engines look for Web pages that have the information you seek. They look for 'keywords'. The information they will provide will include the address of the Web site and a direct hyperlink to the page (or Web site 'home page') you want.

You may see a hyperlink which says 'visit our virtual shop' but it really is a hyperlink called http://www.homepagename. co.uk./ourshop . Sometimes you can click on an image and it too will take you to a different Web page. This is because your cursor activates the URL and your browser will show the Internet address in your address bar. This will include the protocol being used including Hypertext Transfer Protocol (HTTP) and its subsets (XML, etc). The next part of the address is a second protocol such as WWW, which says this is a World Wide Web (WWW) page, and then will come the name of the site (the domain name). When you delve deeper into the site you will find a forward slash (/) and then some more words. This means that you are looking at the other pages that are inside the Web site; see Figure 6.1 for an example.

This is very helpful to know as you explore a Web site. For example, if you are deep inside a Web site and want to know what content there is in the next page up, you can delete the last words and your browser will find the next page up.

It is also important to know that Web sites are created by these hyperlink references between one page and another and between one Web site and another. When you surf, you look for these addresses, find the site and cream down the wave of information you wanted.

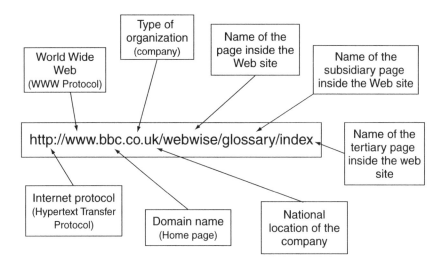

Figure 6.1 *A Web site address*

SEARCH ENGINES

There are many types of search engine and there are a lot of different search engines. You can search different areas of the Internet such as the Web or Usenet (newsgroups), by using different search services. Each service has its own way of compiling and collecting information.

There are two main kinds of search services: the index, and the directory or subject guide.

Indexes

Most if not all of the major search engines attempt to index a representative portion of the entire content of the World Wide Web, using various criteria for determining which are the most important sites to trawl and index. Most search engines also accept submissions from Web site owners. Once a site's pages have been indexed, the search engine will return periodically to the site to update the index. Some search engines give special weighting to words in the title, in subject descriptions and keywords listed in HTML Meta tags, to the first words on a page, and to the frequent recurrence (up to a limit) of a word on a page. Because each of the search engines uses a somewhat different indexing and retrieval scheme (which is likely to be treated as proprietary information) and because each search engine can change its scheme at any time, I do not go into great depth here.

Indexes catalogue words in Web pages and list each page that contains the word(s) you're looking for. They also have the ability to follow any links associated with scanned pages and get even more information. There are billions of Web pages and so catalogues are selective in what they present for you to use. Examples of Indexes are Alta Vista and HotBot.

The job of compiling data for indexes is done by *spiders* (also called *robots*, *bots*, or *crawlers*, ergo the names HotBot and WebCrawler), which is software programmed by humans to automatically gather information from all over the Internet based on specific or broad search criteria. Most of the time spiders scan pages without the owner's knowledge or consent (if you don't want some or all of your Web pages scanned by spiders, you can add a 'robot block' – although many spiders can work round such blocks and some individuals use these technologies to 'hack' sites).

The advantages of this kind of service are that their databases are very large and are updated by spiders working around the clock. The spiders are getting very smart but still return a lot of information that may be a long way from your specific interest.

Directories/subject guides

Yahoo! and Magellan, among others, are hierarchical directories of Web page subjects. Each reference is entered and updated by a person, placing each Web address in a certain context. This is a form of online 'Yellow Pages' but covers a massive range of products, subjects and interests.

When you use these directories, you actually interrogate computer databases for the URL you seek and not the Internet. Typically, indexes point you to Web site home pages rather than the specific page your seek.

To have a Web site listed in a directory you may need to submit it yourself.

Hybrids

Some search services use both methods – they are both an index and a directory – like Infoseek and Excite. These services send out a spider to collect Web site information and also have people cataloguing sites that are submitted by Web developers.

Yahoo!'s directory is one of the best on the Web, but its service is limited. To fill the gaps in its service, Yahoo!! has arrangements with a number of other search engines to provide a wider service.

The most potent hybrids use these combinations in very powerful ways. Special tools let you use a number of search engines at the same time and compile results for you in a single list. These engines are called 'metacrawlers'.

Individual Web sites, especially larger corporate sites, may use a search engine to index and retrieve the content of just their own site. Imagine having a Web site with over a million pages. Just finding information on your own site would be hard without a search engine. The BBC has well over a million pages at www.bbc.co.uk.

There are about 400 search engines available for Internet users and each of them has a specific benefit. Practitioners should become experienced in using several search engines. The Internet has millions of Web sites, billions of Web pages, over a hundred thousand newsgroups and many other properties. Being able to find your way round all this information means that you should keep yourself up to date about the efficacy of different and new Internet search tools.

No one service catalogues the whole Internet. Search engines can be pitifully inadequate, partly because they rely on Web page indexes that were compiled weeks before. It is not just timely material that they miss: pages deep within Web sites are also often missed, as are multimedia files, bibliographies, the bits of information in databases and pages that come in PDF, Adobe's portable document format.

In fact, traditional search engines have access to only a fraction of 1 per cent of what exists on the Web. As many as 500 billion pieces of content are hidden from the view of those search engines, according to BrightPlanet.com, a search company that is seeking to index deep into Web sites. To many search experts, this is the 'invisible Web'; BrightPlanet prefers the term 'deep Web', which it estimates may be 500 times larger than the surface Web that search engines try to cover. Even this extra coverage does not include Web pages that are behind firewalls or are part of intranets.

DIGGING DEEPER INTO THE WEB

To dig deeper into the Web, a new breed of search engine is available that takes a different approach. Instead of broadly scanning the Web by indexing pages from any links they can find, these search engines are devoted to drilling further into speciality areas – medical sites, legal documents, even Web pages dedicated to jokes and parody. Looking for timely financial data? Examples include FinancialFind.com and, FindLaw.com. For the news, http://w.moreover.com and the UK media search engine www.XXX.com are very valuable resources too.

Some select a narrow number of relevant sites and stop at that. They use software agents, or bots that learn not only which pages to search, but also what information to acquire from those pages.

THE INTERNET AS A VIRTUAL LANDSCAPE OF INFORMATION

We now know that the Web is not as well connected as many believe. IBM Research, Compaq Corporate Research Laboratories and AltaVista Company 'mapped' the World Wide Web, and uncovered divisive boundaries between regions of the Internet that make navigation difficult or, in some cases, impossible.

Previous studies, based on small samplings of the Web, suggested that there was a high degree of connectivity between sites. Contrary to those preliminary findings, the study (based on analysis of more than 500 million pages) found that the World Wide Web is fundamentally divided into four large regions, each containing approximately the same number of pages. The findings further indicate that there are massive constellations of Web sites that are inaccessible by links, the most common route of travel between sites for Web surfers. The 'Bow Tie' Theory explained the dynamic behaviour of the Web, and yielded insights into the complex organization of the Web (see Figure 6.2).

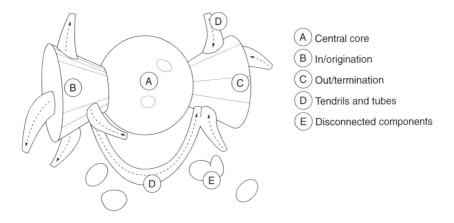

Figure 6.2 *The 'Bow Tie' Theory*

THE BOW TIE

For more information on the 'Bow Tie' theory visit the IBM site at: http://www.almaden.ibm.com/cs/k53/www9.final/.

The results are backed up by the work that Web search company Inktomi has done on indexing the links between pages. Inktomi has indexed around 1.4 billion Web pages to get a better idea of which pages come up as a result of a Web search.

There are varying levels of visibility of Web sites and pages on the Internet.

The so-called 'invisible Web' is information that search engines cannot or refuse to index because it is locked up within databases and is not accessible until the information is pulled up by the user.

There is also what is described as a 'shallow Web'. These are ordinary Web pages that are served out of database systems. They are essentially normal, static pages and belong as part of the surface Web. However, search engines are generally fearful of indexing these because it's easy for them to accidentally index the same page over and over, because the URL might be slightly different due to different features of the dynamic delivery system.

More and more of the surface Web is slipping into the shallow Web, as Webmasters make use of more advanced document delivery tools.

HOW TO SEARCH

The key to searching the Web is not how much you can find, because there is far too much about just about every subject. The important thing is the relevance of what you can find in the time you have available.

This chapter can only point you in the right direction and then it is important to try the range of services that are available. You will find that it is worth having a folder in your browser's 'favourites' or 'bookmarks' with a selection of the search engines you find best. This means that you can use different engines to get to the information you need even when your first choice search engine fails you.

First of all you must decide if the Internet is the best place to find the information you seek. One of the most effective search engines is the telephone. Call the company switchboard and ask for their Web site address. It's a quick, cheap and reliable source of information.

Searching the Internet requires discipline. It is very easy to become distracted by something 'interesting'. To be good at searching the Internet you have to stay focused. Be specific about your purpose and what you want to find. Use the 'favourites' facilities or software to store the relevant information that you want to go back to. The next thing to remember is not to believe everything you see, a subject dealt with in some detail in Chapter 8. You are searching a global resource: the information can be from anywhere and from anyone.

There are three sources that you may like to explore: Web sites, Usenet and Chat. Web sites are found using search engines. Usenet is found using the network and initially Dejanews (www. dejanews.com) is a helpful start. Chat is found in networks such as IRC, ICQ or on individual Web sites (IRC can be monitored in real time at e-Now).

Searching the Web

The simple way to search is to use the 'find' or 'search' facility provided by your service provider. Simply putting in a keyword will produce a list of results.

An enhanced session may use a big search engine like Yahoo! (www.yahoo.com or www.yahoo.co.uk). A simple search on Yahoo! begins by typing in a keyword. Yahoo! first searches its own hierarchically structured subject directory and gives you lists of related directories, Web sites and Web pages. Then, it provides links provided by the AltaVista list and the Google crawler and it also launches a concurrent search for entries matching your search argument with six or seven other major search engines. You can link to each of them from Yahoo! (at the bottom of the search result page) to see what the results were from each of these search engines.

A significant advantage of a Yahoo! search is that if you locate an entry in Yahoo!, it's likely to lead you to a Web site or entire categories of sites related to your search argument. The drawback with a simple keyword is that it is not very specific and will return a lot of sites that require endless reviews to find the information you seek. You need intelligent agents to help.

Searching the Internet needs to be done in a logical way. The names of these logical processes include Boolean, Set, Bayesian, Fuzzy and Neural Networks. Sometimes these are used in combination. In addition, because there is so much information, there is software that can be configured to dig deeper called data-mining software.

Most search engines provide a number of different ways to search. Each one is different. Time well spent is to look at the 'help with searching' or 'advanced' or 'advanced searching' facilities provided by each search engine.

ADVANCED SEARCHING

Yahoo! provides what it calls 'Advanced search'. This comprises the following options and will make your search more effective. Select a search method:

1. Intelligent default

---

2. An exact phrase match
3. Matches on all words (AND)
4. Matches on any word (OR) Select a search area –
5. Yahoo! categories or Web sites.

Even so, such a search may not be very precise and so Yahoo! offers added facilities to help narrow your search. The most powerful searching tool it offers is the application of a technique to allow you to logically add or eliminate specific keywords. The most common logic used by search engines is one of the forms of Boolean syntax searches. These logical forms of search, called operators, allow you to use expressions to put keywords together. These operators include: ADD (a word), OR (use one word instead of another), AND (to include another word) and so forth. Sometimes the search engines require you to use symbols such as attaching a + to a word, which asks for that word be found in all of the search results.

Yahoo! (www.yahoo.co.uk) has an online tutorial for searching. It is replicated here for those who want a book in one hand and a hand spare for the keyboard:

compare: police versus police +sting
Attaching a – in front of a word requires that the word not be found in any of the search result.
compare: python versus python – monty
You can often restrict your search. In Yahoo!, for example, you can use:
t: will restrict searches to document titles only
compare: joe boxer versus t:joe boxer
u: will restrict searches to document URLs only
compare: intel versus u:intel
Putting quotes around a set of words will only find results that match the words in that exact sequence.
compare: great barrier reef versus 'great barrier reef'
Attaching a * to the right-hand side of a word will return left side partial matches.
compare: cap versus cap*
You may combine any of the query syntax as long as the syntax is combined in the proper order.

There are some interesting short cuts. You may want to look into several sites from a single search result. By 'right clicking' on the first desired site and selecting 'Open link in new window' your browser will open a second page and let you select between the two sites that are now open. Using two pages (and more bandwidth) you can search using two search engines at the same time.

SURFING TOOLS

Internet surfing tools include WebFerret (from http://www.softferret.com – an online service) and Intelliseek (http://www.intelliseek.com – a downloadable and heavyweight program). Another example is: http://doc.altavista.com/adv_search/ast_toc.html.

A listing of search engines is available from Searchengine watch at: http://www.searchenginewatch.com/links/ or Websearch at http://Websearch.about.com/internet/Websearch/msubmenu12.html.

For more extensive and specialist search engine information try: http://www.zdnet.com/searchiq/new.

To manage your bookmarks and track searches there is software such as Surfsaver (http://www.surfsaver.com/).

Sophisticated search products are available such as Autonomy (http://www.autonomy.co.uk). You can find the most searched for terms at http://www.searchterms.com/index.html.

Using these simple-to-learn techniques will help you to find more exactly what you need and save a lot of time.

There are a lot of search engines that are specialist and some are very powerful. Some are limited to national, industry or type of Web sites and are ideal for specialist searches.

Searching the newsgroups

Contrary to the name, there is actually very little 'news' in the newsgroups. There is a lot of opinion and comment and more than a little 'insider knowledge', which is why they are so powerful in shaping opinion.

Depending upon your online service or Internet Service Provider (ISP), you should have access to about 12,000 newsgroups (of 100,000 well-documented ones). With this many newsgroups there is probably at least one out there for everyone.

Usenet, the international newsgroup network, is much like the Internet itself: no single agency is in charge. The system connects computers from around the world and the system administrators decide which newsgroups to supply. Very few systems supply all of the newsgroups. An easy introduction to online discussion lists can be found at www.dejanews.com.

Searching newsgroups usually has two types of search: simple search, which accepts some simple Boolean questions, and advanced search, which will accept complex Boolean.

The practitioner may want to create a newsgroup information resource, or the consultancy client team or in-house department may like to create one that can be shared.

ONLINE SEARCH AIDS

Using an online service for saving searches and searched details you can use tools such as those available at: http://www.surf-saver.com/ and http://www.kaylon.com/power.html.

To capture information about a Web site you may like to review e-catch at: http://www.ecatch.com/index.htm.

For more help, try http://www.internet-gopher.com/toolkit.

Using the facilities available in Dejanews or AltaVista, create a personal account. Use the 'advanced' facility to create a search term for the client/client's industry or sector/competitors and set it up in your personal account. Bookmark this page in your Web browser. In this way you will be able to see all the current discussion in a range of newsgroups that affects the client/organization day by day.

More sophisticated searching, and making searches available to the department or the whole enterprise, allows you to share knowledge and provide a new form of 'news and interest from the Net'.

Searching the chat

The most common types of chat are IRC, Webpage (Java) Chat, and ICQ Chat. Each has very good search capability, which is explained in detail.

The drawback with monitoring chat is that there are more than

100,000 people online chatting at any given hour, 24 hours a day, on IRC alone. Monitoring ephemeral chat is notoriously difficult and keeping the information for analysis is virtually impossible at the time of writing – but lots of people are working on it.

Saving searches

When saving searches, you will need to decide what you need to keep.

You will have to decide what subjects you will cover. It may be that you want to identify Internet properties for yourself, for your work group or department, or for the whole organization. You may even be searching for properties where the knowledge can be shared with external publics such as journalists. If this is so, what will be your guiding rules? You may like to look at Chapter 9 (Creating resources for Internet users).

Saving content

Once you have found the information needed, there are a number of options for its management:

1. Save the site, page or URL.
2. Print.
3. Send the page or URL to a third person (who must also have a browser that has the same or fewer security restrictions – firewalls, security settings).
4. Bookmarks (and it is very sensible to organize them).

Use a software program to download and browse your selected Web sites. Browse offline and trace changes (updates, search and advanced highlighting functions) and carry out advanced text searches, export Web sites, or download selected links while you are reading the pages offline. Saving Usenet searches is a facility available on both Dejanews and Altavista and can be both historic and can be maintained up to date.

Learning to surf the Internet may seem like a breeze, but it's not! Learning to use different search engines and their capabilities, and becoming really effective, takes time. The payoff is huge. You get better-quality information faster and more reliably every time and you are effective every time you have to do any research for your organization. Surfing well gets you to the top of the wave.

7

Mapping and monitoring your presence in cyberspace

You don't need to be a white water surfer to be aware of the nature of Internet constituent views and interests. You will already know about lots of sites your friends and colleagues have pointed out that mention your organization.

As in all life, knowing precisely what the whole world thinks and says about an organization is a tough call. The volume of information now available across the Internet is too great for constant monitoring without powerful monitoring tools.

In principle there are three forms of Internet intelligence gathering. They are used to identify Internet constituents:

1. Landscaping.
2. Auditing.
3. Monitoring.

LANDSCAPING

Landscaping is the process of finding the Web sites, discussion lists and other Internet resources that provide information about your organization (and more elaborately, your industry sector or akin organizations). It will identify the properties (and type of properties) where your organization is evident, the nature of the content such as corporate and personal Web sites, Web pages, newsgroups, discussion lists, bulletin boards and online media. The nature of the content is analytically described. Practitioners can landscape the Internet to a certain degree with software tools. These will list Web sites and (to a limited extent) newsgroups and online new media.

Newsgroup research can be undertaken using www. dejanews.com and www.altavista.com, etc. For many applications such research is quite adequate but there is a good case for using expert capability and the many powerful software and Internet tools they can deploy. This analysis provides information on how big the virtual landscape is (how many Internet properties reflect interest in your organization), the extent to which these are interlinked, the subject matter most apparent and its nature. This provides a map of what is being said and where.

LANDSCAPING TOOLS

You can use tools such as Bulls Eye from Intelliseek (http://www.intelliseek.com/).

There are also specialist companies: Infonic (www. infonic.co.uk) identifies, analyses and reports on Internet presence; also check out IRSL (www.netreputation.net). Dr Roger Trobridge (http://www.internet-gopher.com/index.html), provides bespoke research.

Advanced forms of opinion landscaping will identify the most significant subjects and issues in different forms of Internet presence such as news sites, personal sites, corporate sites, discussion lists, newsgroups, etc. This approach will identify and locate the Internet agenda.

The subjects and issues available to the Internet constituent will reflect different interests, issues and concerns. In some instances, organizations' Web sites will be completely out of step with the media and newsgroup agendas, often meaning that they are not responsive to the interests and concerns of the Internet publics.

To gauge the extent to which your organization's agenda is in tune with other interests and views is more complex and requires the use of content or semantic analysis, which can be undertaken in-house or by using specialist services. This form of analysis can be used for a range of PR activities.

Knowing the interests and opinions of Internet consumer constituents may change the whole marketing approach for online presence including the design and content of your Web site/s. The issues discussed or information published may impact on issues management, community affairs, employee relations and the many other forms of PR practice.

The Internet landscape

Landscaping also provides the information needed to identify the significance of different Internet properties. It assists in building lists of important and opinion-forming Web sites.

Included in this research you will want knowledge about views and information concerning products or services, their means to markets and after-sales support, corporate fidelity, employees, and external stakeholders relationships.

AUDITING

The process of auditing Internet presence covers a number of areas and is frequently integrated with landscaping (see Figure 7.1). It is an essential research requirement prior to launching a Web site. It is the means by which you can benchmark your online presence.

Auditing typically covers 11 areas of research:

1. Evaluation of how the organization's competitors are using the Internet and how the organization can uniquely differentiate itself in the online arena.
2. Assessing pre-existing online references and discussions related to the organization. A sudden change in approach may be relevant or can be at odds with Internet constituents' understanding of the organization/sector/context.

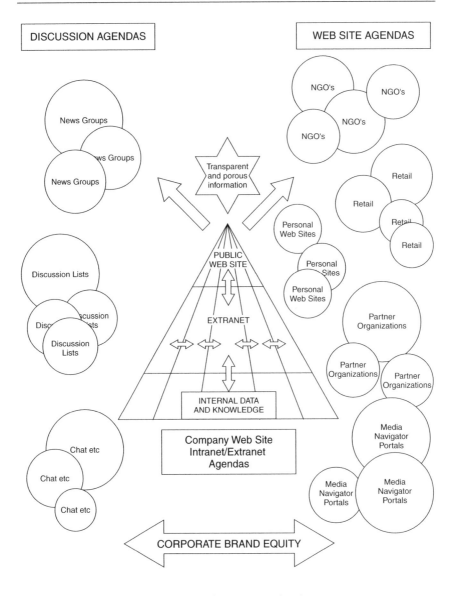

Figure 7.1 *The Internet landscape*

3. Reviewing preconceptions and expectations related to the organization's Internet activities.
4. A planned strategy for integrating the organization's online activities.

5. Analysis of the organization's Web site as a means of building a relationship with local, national and global constituents.
6. Assessing data and network security related to the organization's use of the Internet. The damage to reputation when security is breached or information is inadvertently made available to the public is very significant.
7. Specifying concrete criteria and a process for measuring and evaluating the results of the organization's online activities, for example return on investment, promotion cost/site traffic ratio, revisits and visitor retention, visitor activity (enquire, buy, inform, download, etc).
8. Policies for employee use of Internet assets, along with procedures for making and approving enhancements and revisions to the organization's Web site.
9. Efficacy of procedures for responding to inquiries received via the Internet and evolution of growing and personalized interactivity.
10. Budgets and schedules for implementing the organization's Internet activities.
11. How your organization lives up to expectations and the extent to which it is or can be transparent about its many operational practices.

You may also want to assess and evaluate competitor and other Web sites; Chapter 8 deals with the processes you may want to deploy.

Perceptions

There are always preconceptions of an organization if only as part of the industry sector or the nature of the organization's competitors. These perceptions provide the basis for online presence such as Web sites and also provide the basis for online and offline public relations. Changing online perceptions among a range of Internet constituents has a powerful effect on relationships and reputation because it feeds both online and offline opinion and attitudes. The medium of the Internet is open to continuous flow of opinion-forming information. This flow of information is not controlled and is dynamic, which offers considerable scope for PR activity.

Integration audit

The numbers of cases where there is conflicting information between online and offline activities is endless. In addition it is common to find online partners are a long way behind the times.

AUDIT TO SUSTAIN REPUTATION

On 2 February 2000 when BT announced 3,000 redundancies (see Chapter 4), its online recruitment partner Monster.co.uk was advertising 1,000 jobs and at the same time, BT's Web page about corporate vision was down. This form of inconsistency is typical, avoidable and a PR issue. The audit will expose third party partners and their content. It will also reveal corporate content and brand information. Integrated communications strategy is essential. Auditing who your online information partners are can be a prolonged process for some organizations.

Not managing your online information partners can cause great mirth. The British government's Department of Trade and Industry is trying hard to promote e-commerce. The office of the e-envoy, reporting directly to the Prime Minister, had a six-month old 'What's new page' on 2 February 2001, and a page listing 37 high-powered mandarins, so-called 'Information Age Government Champions', did not work for weeks. The day that Andrew Pinder was appointed e-envoy the press release identified the role of the e-envoy as:

- to galvanize business in the UK to face up to the challenges of e-commerce;
- to provide strategic input into the development of e-government;
- to promote the UK's e-commerce strategy abroad;
- to ensure that the benefits of e-commerce are spread throughout society.

The Internet can be so cruel, but such case studies do bring home the need for audits.

Community building

The extent to which an organization contributes to online and off-line communities and has an integrated approach should be researched. A simple audit of these relationships will identify a wide range of opportunities to build relationships and lever up online brand equity.

Research into interaction between online communities and competitors will also reveal where competitors seek to partner with Internet constituency sympathies.

Security

The security audit of an organization's site is as important as the company fire drill and should be checked at least each week. In addition there should be a direct reporting and issues management structure in place for any compromise in the system.

Competitor security is also an issue. The fallout from one organization to another is significant and competitor liaison is important and should be audited. In my view any security compromise should immediately invoke an exchange of telephone calls from the organization's CEO to all its competitors. It's not that security breaches do not happen or will not happen but that the issues management preparations should be very well honed and the buck stops at the head of PR, the CEO.

Policies for employees

Education, motivation and clear standards of behaviour are essential for all online activities. The way organizations expose themselves via the Internet reflects on all employees and the organization as a whole. Benchmarking Internet knowledge, from e-mail security and disclosures to abuse of facilities, will affect reputation and relationships. There are any number of devices that can be implemented and rules that can be created, but by far the most important audit will be based on levels of understanding of the nature of global 24-hour exposure via the Internet, and on corporate culture. Most employees do not want to compromise the jobs or reputation of colleagues.

The structures in place for managing continually changing Web site content and Internet relationship management need to be thorough. Who, how and when people enhance your Web site and involve third parties need regular auditing.

Responding to inquiries

Every few weeks new research is published which identifies how even the major companies and organizations lack the capability to respond to enquiries and interact with Internet constituents. People are snubbed by companies at their peril. The ability to be able to respond responsibly, effectively and, importantly, fast should not be an issue but must be measured, and a path for enhancing this process identified with measurable improvements designed into the process. Interaction with Internet constituents is the stuff of success.

Budgets

Never mind 'new economy' funny money. When it comes to Internet budgets, return on investment and financial probity, Web site development has to obey some pretty old-fashioned rules. Good estimating, effective buying, cost control and measurable performance apply to the Internet as much as to other forms of governance. The extent of available expertise is such that estimates and costs can be identified easily and they must be adhered to. Out of control expenditure in the name of the Internet is not an option.

The timescales for investment and implementation are short and the payback is swift. It is better to achieve limited goals on time and on budget than to try to achieve everything at once. A big Internet project over many months may well be out of date and out of control if it has a long horizon. A strategy may stretch out for a long time but delivery has to be accomplished with tactical achievements.

Always look for the added payback. For example, if the tactic is to implement a monitoring service, can the resulting intelligence also be used in added knowledge for product development, news services for the Web site, identifying new markets, development of additional online partnerships and other commercial advantages? In this way the payback is faster and the value added is greater. A simple analysis of the extent to which Internet-related costs and investment have been assessed for added value opportunity pays handsome dividends.

Auditing the creative deployment as well as project management mean that the organization will be more effective and competitive.

Living up to expectations

The expectations of the Internet constituents, the organization's management and employees have to be continuously measured. Identifying the ambitions of constituents and then exceeding expectations bring high returns and considerable rewards.

MONITORING

It is not possible to monitor the whole Internet. There are billions of Web pages, tens of thousands of Newsgroups, untold bulletin boards, endless instant messages and mountains of e-mail. In addition, there is streamed news, video, music and ticker, which may be vital to commerce or never called upon by the Internet population.

There is information that is transitory (shallow Web). This can be the passing information flashed up via a Java script or MUD event and is then lost forever. In addition there is information that is available by activating organization's databases, which may be specific to the tiniest minority of surfers (online data mining of corporate databases). This adds massively to the knowledge available but requires interactive effort (deep Web).

It is possible to monitor individual Web pages and Web sites using online services. These services will both aid research into individual sites and identify changes as they occur. Other services monitor other sites such as the streamed new services. It is possible to track a lot of the Internet in this way, but it is very time-consuming. This is a case of working out if you want to spend most of your time searching for information and news or more of your time acting on the intelligence derived from searching the Internet. The cost of using an online service, the technologies that can be deployed and added management of citations (clippings) are all important considerations.

The monitoring companies do not provide historic information. That will be included in landscaping. They look at what is new each day and report their findings (usually via e-mail alert and a password-protected Web site). These services use heavyweight search robots and look at the Internet in four ways:

1. They have an index (catalogue) of news sites and online e-zines which they search each day.
2. They search an index (catalogue) of newsgroups and bulletin boards.
3. They search (catalogues of) selected and publicly available bulletin boards.
4. They use Meta search engines to find out what relevant content has been indexed in the previous day (remembering that search engines can take up to six weeks to re-index sites to find the latest additions and subtractions from sites).

The coverage of these services is high and though not comprehensive (nothing is), represents exceptional capability. The better services search the core several million Web sites (and most of their pages), 100,000 newsgroups and most online publications in the EU and the United States every day, and dwell in each site for often half an hour at a time seeking out the relevant details.

E-mail, chat and Web-enabled telephony are not monitored. There are software packages that companies use to monitor exchanges between employees and between employees and external publics. Even so, the volume is so high that other forms of tracing are needed before such software is of real value.

Most organizations are unaware of the amount of information that is posted about them each day. For some, the levels are very high – Microsoft as a generic search would provide too many returns to be manageable.

This means that monitoring may have to be made quite specific. Searching can be for the organization as a whole, for a brand, issue, or subject.

The use of powerful searching syntax is helpful as the big problem is not how little attention an organization will receive across the Internet but how much and how relevant. It often pays to split searches into specific subjects, which is possible both automatically and manually using the better monitoring services. This means that relevant information can be stored, indexed, searched and analysed as well as being shared across the enterprise.

When deploying a monitoring service, best practice will look at where, besides the PR department, this source of information will

---

MONITORING RESOURCES

Online monitoring services for individual Web sites include Mind-it http://mindit.netmind.com and e-Catch http://www. ecatch.com.

The more significant Internet monitoring companies are: http://www.cyberalert.com/, http://www.durrants.co.uk/ http://www.tellex.press.net/
http://www.romeike.com/netcuthome.htm
http://www.clippingservice.com/, http://www.ewatch.com/ and http://www.Webclipping.com

Yahoo!'s list of online monitoring resources is at http://dir.yahoo.com/business_and_economy/business_to_business /corporate_services/public_relations/clipping_and_monitoring_ services/.

---

be useful and helpful. Intelligence about competition, new processes and products, original research, use and abuse of intellectual property, financial news, government regulation, law suites and much more can be channelled to a range of departments to add to their knowledge and capability. For example: to make available the vast majority of product development information across the Internet to the Research and Development department for £2,000 per year is a real bargain and can be part of the PR department's service in providing enterprise-wide knowledge resources.

The monitoring organizations have sophisticated search capabilities and many have effective (and necessary) citation management capabilities.

8

Evaluating Internet properties

You have to know about people and organizations before you can build relationships with them and this is as true in cyberspace as in Cardiff.

Your ambition may be to make friends, create a mutually advantageous commercial arrangement or to put right a misapprehension. Until you know who's at the other end, you are at a disadvantage. The people on the Internet come in all forms, shapes, cultures and opinions. Every Web site is unique. They look different; have different content and different navigation. They vary in what they say. Some are not as fresh as they might be! Others are or just look tired and out of date or old.

Usenet newsgroups are made by personalities too. This means that each newsgroup has a personality reflecting its members and within each newsgroup there are unique characters and contributors.

It can similarly be said of other forms of Internet communication that they too have unique attributes. Because of this those of us who wish to have a relationship in cyberspace with any public need to understand the importance of lurking, netiquette and researching into the nature and background of Web sites and Internet presence.

Unlike other forms of PR where there may be some leeway as to whether evaluation is absolutely critical or not, there is no option but to investigate Web presence before you do anything. The *Financial Times* has a different editor between the on and off-line versions. As a result, one needs a sense of the difference between the printed version of the *FT* and its online cousin.

In the same way that a practitioner would not attempt to provide editorial content to a newspaper or magazine without first reading it, the same is true of Internet presence. This means that the practitioner needs some way to assess or evaluate every Internet presence he or she wishes to influence.

Elsewhere in this book you will be encouraged to pass on information about Web sites to help work colleagues, other departments or even a complete company. In addition you will seize the opportunity to enhance the content of articles and briefing documents by presenting information from reliable Internet sources. In fact, you have probably done this already.

It is pretty obvious that you will want to present the very best information that will give you a competitive edge and an advantage from the knowledge you have gained via the Internet. To be able to pass on such knowledge and enhance the work you offer to third parties (such as journalists), you need to be assured that the information you add is nothing but the best. To be able to achieve this the practitioner needs to be very proficient in evaluating Web sites and Internet presence.

EVALUATING WEB SITES

Exploration requires a large dose of common sense, a structured approach and some knowledge of the technologies that are available to help. Alternatively, the job can be passed to an expert in the field.

To be able to build any form of serious or sustainable relationship, this background work just has to be done. Jumping into a relationship with a Web site without proper investigation is just asking to get hurt. More than a few Web sites are, at face value, respectable, even fun places to visit and to build into a communi-

---

MONITORING HYPERLINKS AND SEARCH ENGINE RANKINGS

The amount of software and online services available to help you is staggering; here are some starting points.

(http://Websitegarage.netscape.com/) shows which hyperlinks are failing and also shows comparative search engine rankings.

For Web site traffic statistics, visit http://www.watchfire.com/, http://www.nielsen-netratings.com/ or http://www.mediametrix.com/.

---

cations strategy. Not infrequently, they have no substance or a very dubious background.

The process for evaluating a Web site has five key elements: information about the site, the site content, the site reach, its constituents, and the relationships it enjoys (empathy). We will deal with each in turn.

To build your own evaluation process, a simple checklist and even marks out of 10 for the points identified below will be sufficient for many, if not most preliminary evaluations. As we all know, time is a real problem and so it is important to automate the process and make it fast and efficient.

You can use this kind of Web site analysis on your own site, on competitors' sites, and for evaluation and analysis of third party sites.

ABOUT THE SITE

When looking at a site for the first time there are some questions that automatically come to mind, such as what is the quality of site construction in terms of layout, navigation, design, spelling or even broken links (see Figure 8.1).

To be sure about a site we need to know who owns it (and how to contact them) and, being social animals, we like to know if it has lots of contributors and enthusiasts or if it is a brave individual putting all under the public eye, ready for bombardment by e-mails, discussion, consumer comments and third party contributions. Our aim is to see if this Webmaster and site champion are competent.

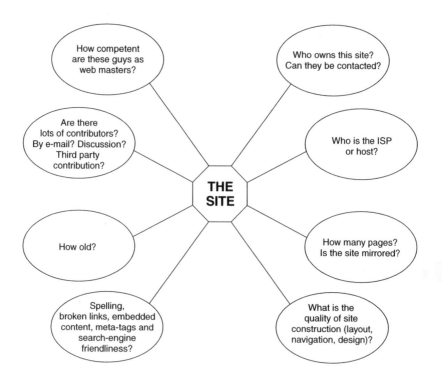

Figure 8.1 *The construction of a Web site*

You may be looking at a site because you want to build a relationship with its owner or its constituents. You may want to know about a site because it is being nasty to you, so you may want to look further.

THE CONTENT

Like people, every Web site is different. Some of the content can be fun or hazardous and you can make some pretty accurate judgements. However, even today, there are large organizations that are pretty slow at updating their sites. Some big retailers even have Christmas offers still on their site in February but would not dream of leaving their shop window unattended for three months.

There is always a reason for someone building a Web site. Some sites are just an ego boost but others have very defined objectives, which can be anything from selling, buying, entrepôt, auction, information, advertising, fun, knowledge, academic, parody or spoof, criticism, rant or, quite often, close argument. Sites address

Anatomy of a Web site (richness)

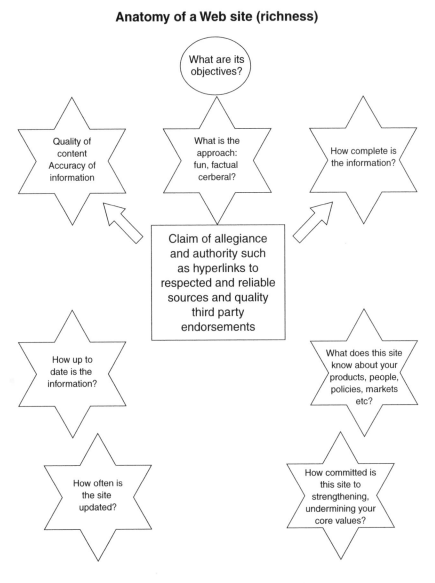

Figure 8.2 *The anatomy of a Web site*

issues and have different approaches. It is not uncommon to see third party (even your own) content and arguments, logo, copyright words, images, sound, video or even patents plagiarized. With some luck, there will be hyperlinks to your site and (unlucky) some may not be the links you desire!

Looking at other people's sites, you might ask about the quality of its own and other people's content or arguments. Who are their information sources and where does the site claim its allegiance and authority, such as hyperlinks to respected and reliable sources and quality or third party endorsements?

Lots of sites are a dead end (a 'push' site), which is boring and for some, the information is inaccurate, incomplete, out of date and unchanging. Some sites are a front for another organization and others have more cheering links to affiliates and third party virtual partners (this can be a news feed or search facility or it might be another company or product and, of course, may be banner advertisements).

One may ask of a site you are interested in whether its owners know about your people, policies, processes, markets, Internet constituents and if there is such a link, is this a cry for involvement, help, attention, and/or retribution? The bottom line is whether this site represents the most advanced information, knowledge, reasoning, products or pricing across the whole of the Internet. In other words, is this a world-competitive knowledge resource?

REACH

Of course, when you look at a Web site, you will be curious as to how many people see it and, more important, revisit.

This is a tough one but not as tough as it may seem. The very big sites are measured by pollsters asking about sites people use, but most sites are not the BBC or Yahoo! In many cases, the practitioner has to be something of a detective to identify the extent to which a site is popular, but can get a very good idea from observations in cyberspace. Web sites give off lots of clues about their reach. Some are referenced newsgroups and discussion lists and there is an online community interested and reacting for or against the content.

The links into and from other sites are significant and media

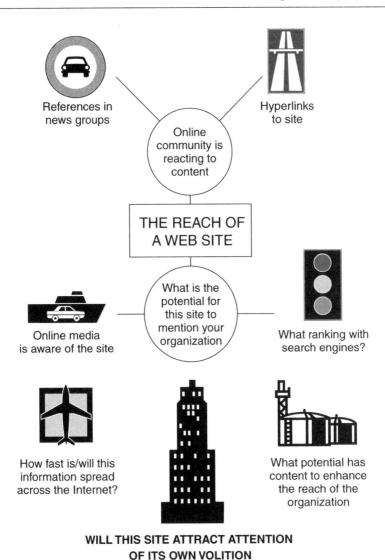

References in news groups

Hyperlinks to site

Online community is reacting to content

THE REACH OF A WEB SITE

What is the potential for this site to mention your organization

Online media is aware of the site

What ranking with search engines?

How fast is/will this information spread across the Internet?

What potential has content to enhance the reach of the organization

WILL THIS SITE ATTRACT ATTENTION OF ITS OWN VOLITION

Figure 8.3 *The reach of a Web site*

awareness is important too. But you may like to ask more open-ended questions about reach, such as whether there is room for the issues on the site to take hold and how fast this information spreads across the Internet.

Sites will have a big presence if they have a good ranking with search engines and with specific types of engines such as crawlers

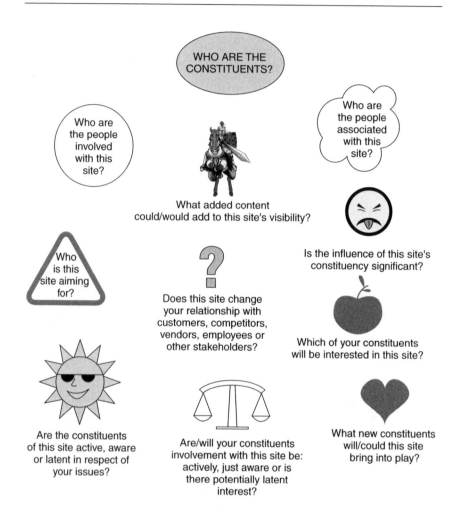

Figure 8.4 *Identifying the constituents for a Web site*

or specialist directories and lists. Of course, if a site owner is good at promotion, this will help too.

Access to this kind of information requires the application of appropriate technologies. At the time of writing a number of technologies is available and more come on stream all the time. In addition, a number of research establishments have been looking at the relationship between Internet presence and behavioural change, which will be of considerable interest to the PR profession.

CONSTITUENTS

With a good idea about the content and visibility of the site, it is very important to know who would be interested in its content and whether their interest will mean they will come back. Indeed, will they come back often or just occasionally? (see Figure 8.4).

If you are to have any relationship with this site, it is very important to know who this site will influence. Looking at Web sites one may ask if its constituents are active, aware or latent (see Chapter 10) and which of your constituents will be interested. Are your constituents active, aware or latent users of this site, what associated issues are likely to be involved and will they add impetus to the site's visibility?

For some sites (such as media and other opinion-forming sites) you will want to take a view about what new constituents they will/could bring into play.

EMPATHY

The effect of a site on its visitors and any consequential effect on your organization or online presence are obviously significant to your organization. This could be a ringing endorsement, a criticism, a navigator to information or call to action.

The thought and evaluation you may need to put into assessing a site may be quite extensive and its ability to generate empathy will be significant. The most obvious question will be whether this site changes your relationship with customers, competitors, vendors, employees, authorities or other constituents. You may also ask if there are opportunities for using endorsements available on this site for your advantage of if there is the means for bringing your critics on side.

The other questions could focus on whether this site is going to affect your core constituents now, soon or slowly and where there is an opportunity for adding to your reputation and relationships with these Internet constituents (see Figure 8.5).

For some sites you may be interested in how you will manage/provide an escape route for the site owner if he or she is a critic, as we discuss Chapter 17.

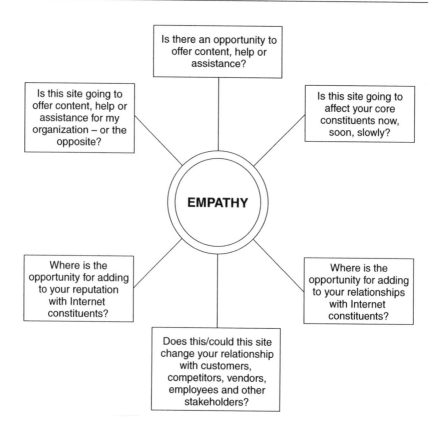

Figure 8.5 *Assessing your Web site*

EVALUATING NEWSGROUPS

Newsgroups, bulletin boards and chat sites can also be evaluated. The practitioner can ask a range of questions of a conversation in cyberspace or the site where a conversation is, has or could potentially take place as part of a relationship management audit. This can be to both promote and defend a corporate reputation.

There are some simple technical questions that one might ask, and an evaluation of the site itself will be helpful. The frequency of use and the number of different users will be of interest. The range of topics discussed and the type of discussion will be important. One may ask: does the site owner moderate the exchange?; is there potential for insensitive responses?; is there time to get to know the newsgroup's culture?

The range of discussion and the interactive nature of newsgroups offer the practitioner a continuous litmus test of attitudes and opinions. In the unmoderated areas of the Internet, full of a mix of serious, quirky, straight, misleading, fun and downright malicious content, there is a happy hunting ground for the researcher into the nature of the organization's relationship with these, largely, articulate, educated and wealthy people. The practitioner can apply a range of techniques to evaluate the content of these online exchanges.

There are a number of caveats. Many companies are excited that they are often referred to in newsgroups but fail to realize that this is only on occasion in each newsgroup and that their presence is not very evident for the users of individual newsgroups. The seeding of newsgroups (typically companies trying to add brand information to an online discussion) often fails because there is little content to create an interactive conversation. Newsgroups are conversational.

As with all conversations and unstructured text, this coverage is open to the use of content analysis and, these days, computerized semantic and semiotic analysis, which provides the practitioner with a clear view of the underlying issues or fashionable conversation of the moment.

CONTENT, SEMANTIC AND SEMIOTIC ANALYSIS

Every newspaper and Web site can be analysed to identify its influence on organizations. The modern capability is very powerful and is making some PR work very effective. Resources are available everywhere; here are some helpful starting places.

The most comprehensive lists of content analysis software are seen at:

http://www.intext.de/textanae.htm

http://www.aber.ac.uk/media/Functions/mcs.html

http://www.aber.ac.uk/media/Functions/mcs.html, or

http://www.newcastle.edu.au/department/fad/fi/woodrow/semiotic.htm)

One of the companies working on PR applications of this area of research is www.mediareportnow.com.

This form of evaluation is very powerful for both proactive Internet promotion and the management of issues.

In evaluating newsgroups and bulletin boards, you may also like to identify what kind of things your organization would want to say or do when engaging with the group, remembering that any exchange, whether to the group or one of its participants can, and frequently will, make it transparently available to the rest of the group and the network in general.

IDENTIFYING BEHAVIOURAL CHANGE

The range of motivations for people to use the Internet and add content is as diverse as humanity itself. However, the number of participants is sufficiently large for us to be able to identify the extent to which an organization's Internet presence evokes and provokes activity across the Internet. This makes it possible to identify the extent to which an Internet presence is affecting its constituents. Furthermore, we can identify the type of Internet presence that is provoking the most activity.

KEEPING UP WITH THE CYBERJONESES

The technologies move on quite fast. Many of them are driven by a type of online robot called a 'bot'. These intelligent programmes work very much like people think; there is more about them at: http://bots.internet.com.

For example, an organization or, more likely, an issue, may be the subject of interactivity in online media, e-zines, newsgroups, private Web sites or among the activists. An issue or brand spreading across the Internet can only do so when a person chooses to make it happen. Because there is choice, this kind of activity demonstrates a form of altered behaviour. This means that the organization, brand or issue has provoked a miserable or powerful response. Using relative responses as between, for example, competitors, the analyst can evaluate the effect or effectiveness of the online issue.

This powerful capability to be able to evaluate behavioural change as a consequence of online presence is very significant and is commercially very valuable.

9

Creating resources for Internet users

Already, if you have used the Internet at all, you will have started your collection of interesting, important or valuable Web sites and resources.

You will want to use some or all of the methods identified in Chapters 8 to 10 to search for the most appropriate sites and to ensure that the sites you have identified are only the very best, trustworthy, reliable, stable and reputable.

Assuming that bookmarks you have added to your favourites list are representative of leading edge, most modern and most reliable resources across the Internet, how can you deploy these for best effect? How can you make your investment in time really pay off?

Let us suppose for a moment that your favourites sites include information that would be helpful to other people in your organization, or would be helpful to a journalist. Could your collection become the knowledge resource for the whole organization? It could be a virtual, reliable, modern and empowering virtual library.

In fact, you already provide a massive knowledge base. It is the raft of press releases, backgrounders and picture resources in the media centre. If you can add to that collection a range of Internet resources, lists of organizations (such as online publications) and news outlets covering your stories online, it would be helpful to a lot of people in the company. Suppose you were to make this a resource of information from academics, about government regulation, industry sector associations and such like, it would help you do your job and it would help lots of other people in your organization do their job. It could become the corporate online library. And so it should. The benefits are that your research will be better and faster. More people in your organization will find your work helpful and you will offer them fast, reliable and globally competitive resources.

In addition, you can offer to share some of this information with external organizations to help them promote the interests of your organization. For example, this reliable resource might be shared with your PR, advertising, marketing and other information partners. You could also share the content of this library with potential customers, journalists and vendors. In doing so, you would add to your reputation and make a greater contribution to the competitive advantage of your organization and its stakeholders.

You must have an online resource. You must do the research to find it. By thinking about online resources strategically, you can turn your investment in finding Internet resources into an enterprise-wide investment to the benefit of all. This means you can turn a necessity into a positive and powerful PR benefit.

FIRST STEPS IN BUILDING INTERNET RESOURCES

The best place to start developing online resources is with your use of your bookmark facility on your Web browser. Later on, this information can be transferred to even more powerful software, but you will need to start somewhere.

A typical PR structure will have folders that provide quick links to client/organization – relevant information, different and favourite search engines, news resources, professional practice sites and discussions. In addition it will point to resources you need hour to hour or day to day. You can create a simple directory (using the directory style in Microsoft's Word) or you can build a database, which may be a better long-term option. Alternatively you may like to follow the conventions of a wider standard such as http://dmoz.org. A structure like this will make relevant Web sites, discussion lists and resources easy to find. It also ensures you can stay up to date about the client/organization and its issues on the Internet. It is also worth editing the lists on a regular basis, typically every month.

To be sure that you monitor the most important sites for changes in their content, you will use one of the online Web site monitoring packages. The basic services from these organizations are free and quite adequate to notify you of changes to specific sites or changes related to specific keywords on relevant sites.

If there is standard practice across an agency or in-house department, aggregating this knowledge has big benefits. So it is important to work out departmental rules on the structure for collecting this information. Using the information in Chapters 8 and 9 you can construct such rules (to suit your own organization) to ensure you have a consistent (department/organization-wide) approach to the collection of globally competitive knowledge acquisition.

Extended into the higher level of enhanced Internet PR practice this simple activity becomes a veritable goldmine for the practitioner and the organization. In Chapter 16, 'The Reach of Internet News', where we look at the virtual press office, it will become apparent that the practitioner will find hyperlink resources invaluable in developing relationships with journalists.

There are three aspects to building your own Internet resources. The first is that you can add significant endorsement, third party reference and a reputation as a trusted authority by using the interconnected nature of the Internet. This means that you can add extra information for people to use and can create a presence that makes your brand respected for being reliable, in the forefront of thinking, and your pages worth revisiting.

The second is that you can create a significant, reliable and effective resource for internal constituents to access via your intranet or LAN and may even share this with external extranet constituents. The added benefit is that you will contribute to their productivity as well. Effectively building online resources helps your organization to become globally competitive because its constituents are accessing only the best information and knowledge from all over the world. You will be able to build a research network that will cut time and add value to benefit many PR activities.

Finally, taken to its logical conclusion, the potential is for PR practice to include a significant resource and to encompass much corporate knowledge management.

HYPERLINK LIBRARIES

Your enterprise-wide library of bookmarks has two faces. It is a resource for your organization and it is a resource you can recommend to external Internet constituents. This means that some of the Web sites you have collected in your library of bookmarks can be identified as being suitable for your organization to publicize to external audiences.

There is one other aspect of hyperlinking you can consider at the same time and that is the nature of organizations that recommend your site by creating hyperlinks from their site to yours. Your organization will be using hyperlinks in a variety of ways and so 'outbound' hyperlinks are important to the practitioner. There will be times when you want to send a link to someone. You may want to include a hyperlink in your Web site or virtual press office.

Hyperlinks can be offered to help visitors to a Web site, or to point a journalist to an expert source on the Web, or to assist employees find resources from the intranet. There are many occasions when organizations will want to create hyperlinks to other sites.

When you add hyperlinks to your Web site, to an e-mail or to an instant message, you take on a series of responsibilities and should develop a policy for inclusion. Keeping up standards that will protect and enhance reputation will mean that you take responsibility for the recommended referral.

THINKING THROUGH HOW TO MAKE KNOWLEDGE AVAILABLE

You may want to make information available selectively. For example, you may want the Web sites with online lists of magazines and e-zines to be readily accessed by the PR department. Other sites you may like to make available internally and yet others easily available to external publics as well. That is not to say you will deny access to such information to stakeholders (they

---

can find the information themselves if they have a mind to) but that its presentation is made more evidently visible to relevant audiences. Attempting to deny access (typically with firewalls) tends to create a culture that tries to find ways round such blocks. This is both unhelpful and time wasting or, when it is in stakeholders' own time (60 per cent of Internet activity takes place in the home) to meet very specific and individual interests and enthusiasms – that may easily be a loss to the organization.

Across an organization, the quality and veracity of the information recommended will influence your reputation among all constituents. While you must always add disclaimers, this does not absolve you from being very careful with the information you recommend. Your reputation depends on it.

There is a need for rules and, in addition, you may consider creating an enterprise knowledge centre to assist other employees meet necessarily high standards. Indeed, both by example and through standardized, enterprise-wide procedures, your Internet resource knowledge will improve the quality of information used throughout the organization.

Knowledge management software, corporate libraries, computer data and press centre archives have much in common. Add to this a catalogue of reliable internal and external hyperlinks and an information centre will add to the capability of the organization. It can raise enterprise-wide knowledge by only recommending the very best resources; it can make communication and value-added interaction with stakeholders reliably rich; and the organization will be sought out as an important source of reliable information.

The requirement to be able to include hyperlinked added value information in press releases and a library of recommended sources for journalists is very important. The catalogue proposed here will include such references. Your catalogue may also include all or some of the lists of external constituents assembled by the PR department as it develops techniques to reach out into cyberspace. The techniques used to collect information about sites outlined here will be helpful for adding to your catalogue of recommended hyperlinks.

This seems to be hard work but there are some short cuts. You can deploy a search engine to help your stakeholders search your intranet and Web site and you can make all or part of your content available to the search engine or the general public (bearing in mind that you must consider and take advice on how much this may compromise corporate security and your vulnerability to hacking).

You can also use directory structures to help you develop high-volume, high-quality resources on your own intranet. Because part of your purpose is to make only the best and globally leading information available, such internal resources need to be well managed and their use carefully monitored to identify the information that is most valuable (popular) to various stakeholders.

Creating linkage and referrals

One of the ways a Web site or newsgroup becomes popular is through hyperlinks from referral sites. These links imply that your site is worth visiting and has a unique characteristic relevant to the Internet constituent. It is one of the great strengths of the Internet and is at the same time a potential hazard.

Few organizations track who is adding a hyperlink to their site. It is simple enough. In many instances, organizations seek out other Internet properties that will include such links.

Link popularity has another benefit: several search engines are using it to help rank sites for searchers. Having lots of in-bound links improves ranking. This form of 'popularity' measurement assumes that sites having many links pointing to them must be 'better' than sites that have few such links. This is all part of an approach to evaluate good Web sites, called 'off-site' criteria. Previously, search engines only looked at 'on-site' criteria when ranking search results, ie a site's HTML text and tags.

Link popularity and analysis include factors such as: link penetration – the raw number of sites linking to your site; link quality – a link from Yahoo! is given a high rating while a link from a lesser site is given little or none at all, which factors out useless free-for-all pages of links; topical cross-linking – sites that focus on the same vertical (narrow) topic tend to link to each other.

From an advertising or marketing standpoint, link popularity means that you should make sure your site is linked to and by topical portals, search engines and directories, and exchange links with sites that have similar subject matter as your site (this does not mean affiliate marketing, but simple plain HTML hyperlinks). The software-driven affiliate and (especially) ambassador marketing processes are enormously powerful and drive traffic to sites at an unprecedented rate.

Regardless of whether or not the search engines continue using off-site methods for determining relevancy, you will be building a large network of inbound links that will be there all the time. This has the potential advantage of improved search engine ranking of traffic from the referral sites.

Choosing links

Care should be taken over links. There are some sites and references that you may feel inappropriate to your organization, and the owner of the Web site should be politely invited to remove the link. The rules as to which inbound hyperlinks you prefer to attract are akin to those your organization likes to recommend (see below) and it is easy to adopt the same rules for both. On a more positive note, visitors recommended to your site will be more comfortable and trusting and, where you reciprocate, they respect this attention to their needs for referrals to your trusted partners.

When you provide good referral services, your site can begin to take on aspects of a portal and will attract visitors who use your site as a 'jumping off' point to another property – or if your content appeals at the time, further into your site. In both cases you win with enhanced perceptions of your organization. What you will be doing is helping your organization to recommend Internet properties from your site. But it does not stop there. Lots of people in your organization offer directions to Internet properties.

The Internet is a massive library. Regrettably the content of this library ranges from the most unadulterated rubbish to the most profound additions to human knowledge, and every shade in between. Your job, and the reputation of your organization will depend on it, is to create an environment for only the most reliable sources to be used and only the most expert information be accessed.

In the selection process, the scope of the service will affect the first decisions made about the quality of the resources you will use. Those falling outside the scope will be rejected, and those falling within it will go on through the rest of the selection process, and be evaluated in the light of the rest of the quality criteria. Using the evaluation criteria you have developed (Chapters 8 and 9) you will have a good knowledge of a potential site for use in this type of Internet PR. There are some additional rules you may want to apply.

Selection of subject matter that is only appropriate for the (internal and external) Internet constituents you have in mind is a valid objective. This can be hard to sustain because of the nature of transparency and porosity. In the range of material you may want to acquire and manage for your organization will be subjects that will be censored by you (eg resources produced by hate groups or about bomb-making/paedophilia) and you will want to make this policy transparently available to your constituents.

The other considerations such as the importance of the subject matter to the linked site/s and selection based on information types such as scholarly news or perhaps popular sites including search engines and portals will be significant for different parts of your organization and when recommended to third parties.

Some sites will be recommended because they are directories and others will be included specifically because they are not. You will need to build your own rules (and make them evident to users) about what information you are directing them to.

When deep linking to specific pages or just pointing to sites, you will want to have a view (and process for management) as to whether the site selected is either proven to be, or expected to be, durable.

In selecting sites for your organization or for third party recommendation it is sensible to ask if such a resource is intended for use by an individual, a special interest or local group and whether it is culturally acceptable, offers leading edge or new or controversial developments.

Sources of information

Rules as to which sources of information are acceptable/appropriate for the Internet constituents cover academic, government, commercial, trade/industry, competitor and non-profit and private sources. These can be from individual enthusiasts (for example, fan pages, student pages, enthusiast sites and discussion lists, photo and film libraries) and may be biased, opinionated and ideologically suspect. When these sites are offered to your constituents you will need to be very clear about the conditions that will apply when you offer them.

This thinking will lead you to identifying how you decide what level of resource is appropriate for the Internet constituents (remembering that users may be sensitive employees, school children, journalists, customers, vendors and academics). These decisions may be simple, such as 'Are resources that contain advertising acceptable and are there any forms of advertising which are inappropriate?' to 'Will our links point to free resources or will we include paid-for sites?'

You will sometimes need to decide if you are prepared to pay for licences to offer a gateway to paid-for information and copyright material, and to be able to judge if resources are under copyright or are commercially sensitive. For the budget conscious, will it be costly to sustain, monitor and manage a hyperlink (eg, the URL may change – as it does for many news pages when you deep link into a site)?

When recommending online knowledge to pass on to third parties there is an issue as to what technologies are appropriate for the Internet constituents (forms, databases, Java applications, frames, etc) and what connection speeds are appropriate (pointing a rural UK user to a site best viewed with 56k modem speed, ADSL or ISDN will just add salt to the wound of network inadequacy).

Already many practitioners have bookmarked exciting Web sites they like to recommend. Is online registration or a contractual undertaking (often not very evident to a casual visitor but significant to a commercial site user) acceptable in your catalogue?

There are two other points to consider when building your resource of recommended Web sites and properties. When it is necessary for you to send confidential information over the Internet, will the provision of a secure coding system or encryption affect the selection of the sites you choose to add; and do your constituents have any special needs that will make your selection disagreeable, such as seeing or hearing impediments?

Policy guidelines

Policy guidelines will be needed for where your hyperlink will point. It is possible to point to the home page but if the information is deep inside a big site, you may want to point to a specific site page (deep linking) or newsgroup level, or even a specific citation. You may want to have rules on the minimum amount of information needed for your constituents. Such considerations may include the rules that assure the veracity of the site.

This may seem to be a huge undertaking. For some organizations (a large company department or PR consultancy), the investment will be considerable and the rules will be carefully crafted and applied. For other organizations (and individuals) the range of knowledge they have to share or need to offer will be less extensive and the rules can be more intuitive. In both extremes, it is quite sensible to create a structured catalogue (directory) for your own use or for the organization to access.

To assist in the selection of citations, you may construct your catalogue to have an introduction, or short synopsis describing the content. This will need a standard form (how many words, layout, key points, why the site is important). When cataloguing there are a number of considerations relevant to later use by internal and external constituents.

Is this URL relevant to:

- the whole organization;
- part of the organization;
- a product or service;
- a department;
- a person?

Is the entire selected site relevant:

- from the home page;
- several linked pages;
- a single page?

You may also like to incorporate rules developed from the issues raised in Chapter 8 to identify the kind of site you are adding and the various related attributes of interest or concern.

By having this information available, researching and including content in the organization's enterprise-wide activities, the capability to lever up its benefits to your advantage are greatly enhanced. In larger organizations where knowledge management is more advanced, software is available to help this process; it also provides free-form interrogation of intranets.

This is a significant commitment but the pay-off in terms of being able to offer reliable, informative and reputation-enhancing hyperlinks to internal and external constituents says a lot about the capability of your organization. On a cost for benefit basis, this operation and its maintenance may be equal to a couple of feature articles in the old world, but the benefits can affect both internal and external audiences far more and for much longer.

Automating the process and making it available to internal stakeholders can spread the load. As many employees are engaged in searching the Web and building lists, they can enhance the knowledge library for all, and the cost of acquisition drops rapidly. The key is to be able to develop a set of rules that will apply across the enterprise. This will mean that everyone in the organization will be able to access and rely on this powerful library resource.

This offer will give you a major competitive advantage. Your organization will be better informed and its employees will have world-leading information to deploy. Your work will be globally competitive too and will be respected for its up-to-date and comprehensively sound nature. Organizations and individuals will seek you and your organization as being at the leading edge.

10

Finding partners and enhancing reach

Once upon a time there was the media and media relations was just that. No more! The offline and pre-Internet PR activities, though changed, remain. Now there is a greater range of added communications channels and a wider range of communications methods. In addition to newspapers, posters, radio and television, there are WAP phones, PalmPilots, PCs, information kiosks, SMS and lots more. As communications specialists, the PR community has to find partners in communication.

These partners may continue to be the many news sites, which are akin to online versions of offline newspapers. There are also online media that do not have a printed offline presence (commonly called e-zines) and there is a hybrid. This is an offline newspaper that has an online edition but which also carries news that will not be in the printed publication and may have real-time deadlines, publishing breaking news as it happens online.

In addition there are organization that like to include news to make their Web sites more interesting. There are ambassadors and fans. For example, a football enthusiast with an unofficial club site may like to include breaking news from the club and the league as an added feature for visitors.

In a number of cases trading partners such as retailers, dealers, distributors, agents, and online information partners will welcome content to add to their intranet, Web site or point-of-sale kiosks. Some distributors take real time Internet content for point-of-sale display.

There is a further important group of Web sites that the practitioner has to consider. These are interest sites, which add content to their sites/intranets and extranets because it enriches the experience of their constituents.

All these sites will potentially take your rich content to include on their sites. They seek affinity with your online presence. In a word they have built or seek to build a relationship. This is online PR. Of course this is a two-way street. Practitioners may also find value in accepting content from third parties that will encourage use and enrich their site, intranets and extranets.

PR practitioners now need to be very professional to find sites that will include content from their organization. The opportunity to add your copy and online richness and spread it across more and more sites will make it available to a much wider audience. The high cost of production will be amortized by becoming available to more Web sites and users of the Internet.

There is a process for identifying these sites that allows you to build up your own list of online resources and the contact details that are relevant to these outlets. When building such lists, it is always advisable to keep the online information on a searchable database. The reason is simple. Contacts and journalists can work for a number of Web site owners and Web site owners mix and match in-house and freelance contributors. Web site owners, their Webmasters and the other relevant contacts at an Internet property will have different roles and responsibilities. Being able to search a database is more accurate and saves hours compared to using lists.

In addition, such is the Internet that people can and do work for competitors. Being able to list and reach these people and be relevant to their interests is very important. Searching a simple list for the right contact would probably not immediately throw up such relationships and your targeting can, as a consequence, be inaccurate and, occasionally, dangerous.

There is contact management software available specifically designed for practitioners, which is helpful and can take a lot of the strain and time involved in both developing the lists and maintaining up-to-date information.

FINDING THE SITES

Practitioners will need to develop skills in finding sites. One of the most important applications for these skills will be in developing lists of relevant online publications in exactly the same way that the PR professional finds the addresses and information needed about traditional newspapers and magazines.

There are many ways to find relevant sites. Search engines and landscaping are the most obvious routes, but monitoring will also reveal new Internet properties. Another means for identifying sites is the use of auditing software that will show you who has built hyperlinks to your site. There are also lists that can be bought for almost any subject and there are media list providers to help. Remember that there are other Internet properties that will be important to you such as newsgroups and chat sites.

As we have seen in the preceding chapters, when building lists for information partnership activities you will need to follow well-established and rigorous guidelines and you will need to use contact management software to ensure that you have captured all the information you need *and* be able to retrieve it.

The full force of the Data Protection Act applies in the UK. This means that any list of people or organizations must comply with the provisions of the Act. This is true for lists of UK citizens and for people living overseas.

The processes for identifying relevant sites and journalistic contacts outlined here can also be incorporated into your other forms of Web site resources where your organization wants to build close working relationships. These sites can be even more powerful than media sites for developing online presence.

Many companies have their own means for developing lists of sites they want to cosy up to. Building relationships with other online properties means the practitioner has to follow the general principles for evaluating sites (Chapter 8) because you do not want to be associated with a dubious partner. In addition, there may be some extra information you will want such as:

- Where the content originates. Determine which content is original and which originates at other sites or sources. Knowing where content originates is essential in order to identify the appropriate originator or organization to contact with coverage ideas or press releases.
- How information flows between online and offline sources. Don't assume information that appears in an offline publication or broadcast will make it to the online counterpart, and vice versa.
- The site's refresh and news cycle. Your content, promotion, hyperlink, press release or story idea has a greater chance of being considered when your submission coincides with the site's refresh/news cycle. For media sites, find out the news deadlines. Story lead times vary by site. Some sites cover breaking news, others don't. Some have a mix of non-breaking and breaking news, with different deadlines for each. Non-media sites often have refresh cycles and areas for new or breaking information and news.
- The key contacts at each site. Your content, promotion, hyperlink, story idea or press release are more likely to be read if they are submitted to the right person. You will need the names, e-mail addresses, telephone and (perhaps) fax numbers and contact information for key contacts. These key contacts will include the Webmaster, editors and online content contributors, and the commercial managers responsible for the site.

DIFFERENT MEANS FOR CONTENT DELIVERY

You need an electronic means of submitting material, since the Web, more than any other medium, needs electronic communication. This will include e-mail, Web pages, hyperlinks, digital photographs and logos, software and other ways for building a relationship.

Use the preferred method of contact. Your chances of influencing content and coverage are greatly improved when you approach the appropriate person by the means he or she prefers, whether it's electronic or otherwise. Knowing the preferences of the person you're dealing with enables you to design your submission in a way that will be noticed.

Determine whether the site is a content or news feed for other sites. Coverage at one key site that passes along content to other sites will add reach for your contributions (and may drive even more traffic to your site). This can add circulation and impact for a news story or other piece of information but also may become the channel for confidential or sensitive information to reach beyond your needs. You want to take account of this when deciding which sites to devote your PR resources to.

Look for archival options that could add to the impact of your PR efforts. Coverage of your content or messages on a site that archives its coverage, and makes archived coverage accessible, adds tremendous 'shelf life' to your exposure and could be a factor in planning where to assign resources.

Be prepared to provide rich content. Much online media and many Web sites require considerable added 'richness'. This can include copy presented as headline, synopsis, added background content, logos and photographs, video, sound, interactivity, backgrounders, white papers and hyperlinks (pre-agreed with the site owners and 'other sources') to third party sites. You may need to create briefing Web sites to offer more extensive background information.

Other sites may want different content, live data or information or even video, sound or interactive capability. Be prepared to offer a 'branded service'. This will allow your information partners to add content to their sites without having to reformat it.

This is a very traditional form of 'push' PR. It entails you building relationships with a medium you think is right for you. The Internet is mostly a 'pull' medium with people seeking information and relationships to meet their needs at the time relevant to them. We will look at how this can be accommodated in the next chapter.

FINDING YOUR INTERNET CONSTITUENTS

A significant proportion of Internet presence for many organizations is blurted out without much consideration for the interests or effects on Internet constituents.

A massive, and wasted, effort is put behind 'driving traffic' to Web sites. The interests of the visitors and response to visits, if well thought through, could be a rich invitation to someone who 'wants to visit'. Understanding Internet constituents and going part-way to meet their interests, desires and motivation, offer much more cost-effective and rewarding site promotion and visitor interaction.

The successful communicator will want to create an empathy and mutual magnetic attraction between the organization and its active, aware and latent constituents. The objective is to keep existing relationships alive and fresh, attract the people who know your organization and appeal to the interests of those who, so far, don't know you.

Issues-driven constituents

The people interested in an organization have many and frequently conflicting agendas, which are very evident when analysing the interests of Internet users. In addition, the traditional segmentation of messages to specialist publics/media is not an option when information is made available across the Internet. This means that the principle of separating people into socio-economic groups, consumer profiles, or PR publics is no longer adequate as an aid to communication segmentation. The Internet publics are 'constituents'.

If you cannot segment people into neat marketing boxes, it is quite hard to define their interests. For example, they may be customers but also may be anti-consumerist. This means 'publics' may, at one and the same time, have one issue (eg how can I buy strawberries at Christmas?), which can conflict with another issue (eg how can I stop pollution?)

The marketer may consider a person as a consumer prospect. The prospect knows only that he or she has an issue. Consumers live in a maelstrom of issues. Where do I buy? How much does it cost? How do I decide? How do my actions square up to my ethical beliefs? Can I trust this Web site? Is this online company still fashionable? Is it up to date? Will I look un-cool if I do this? What are the alternatives?

Above the line adverting and below the line promotions, point of sale sales aids and direct marketing are not very interactive, need only pay passing attention to issues and hardly engage the consumer. There is no imperative for the consumer to 'do anything'. With the Internet consumers are already active, engaged and participating. They are using the Internet and need something more than a poster.

The PR practitioner has to identify how to interact with these engaged 'issues-driven Internet constituents'. In Chapter 1 we looked at the motivation of constituents. This gives us the clue as to how we may appeal to online constituents.

WHAT IS AN ISSUE?

When an organization or its publics behave in a way that has consequences for each other, they create issues. Issues can be identified in three ways:

1. People will actively seek information about the issue that concerns them and/or record (or process) information that comes to them unsought.
2. A constraint describes the extent to which people believe there are obstacles that limit their ability to fulfil their plans.
3. 'Level of involvement' means the extent to which a person feels connected to a particular situation and will determine whether he or she is likely to act or not.

Finding where the issues are and what they are requires analysis. The locations can be in any of the properties in the constituents' agenda matrix.

Where the issues are, so are the constituents

Constituent issues will be evident in each of the many types of Internet property. Many Internet properties address many issues. Significantly, the issues may be different between these types of properties. This means that your landscaping will include:

- online editions of media sites (including e-zines);
- the Web sites of competitors and information partners, vendors (and for B2B marketing, customers);
- retailers and other outlet sites;
- personal Web sites;
- government, public sector and academic sites;
- Non governmental organization (NGO) and consumer sites;
- newsgroups and bulletin boards;
- such other outlets as may emerge.

The content from such groups of Internet properties needs analysis to identify the issues that abound and the subjects most in evidence.

Identifying the issues and topics uppermost in the minds of Internet constituents involves finding out where there is mention of the organization and/or subjects related to its activities. For example, a supermarket might look at the subject of supermarkets using a search term that will identify comments about a number of its competitors. Such a search will show where the subject 'supermarkets' is evident in different types of Web site and Internet debate and discussion. Having found the sites where there is commentary, the content can be analysed. It is no great surprise to find that the content in the 'news' sites is different from the 'supermarket' sites. Then again there will be different content in activist and consumer sites. In addition newsgroups and bulletin boards will show/reveal a different type of content. (see Figure 7.1 in Chapter 7). In some cases there will be matching topics but the priority of these topics will be different between the different types of Internet properties.

CONTEXT RELEVANT PRESENCE HAS A MAGNETIC EFFECT

Sabine Geldof at the Artificial Intelligence Laboratory, Vrije Universiteit, Brussels, has been looking at generating text in context and has prepared a number of very good papers and experiments. A relevant paper can be found at: http://arti.vub.ac.be/~sabine/papers/AIX97/paper.html.

The practitioner, having undertaken such research, will be in possession of information about where their sector is evident across the Internet and what the Internet constituents' agenda is for each type of property. This analysis provides the basis for developing a strategic response, internal briefing, message development, Web site design, content and the approach towards different Internet constituents. Once the organization has created its response, it can revisit its landscaping analysis, identify the actual sites/properties for interaction and begin to build relationships and empathy with constituents. This sounds rather like common sense. It is.

The application of advanced research including semantic analysis (the study of the relationships between words and meanings) and related forms of analysis will quickly identify the most relevant constituents' issues.

MEETING YOUR CONSTITUENTS HALFWAY

Applying Internet PR management is not as hard as it seems.

Having completed the research and by knowing where your relevant Internet continents are and what drives them, and the contexts that are relevant to them, there is a simple process for engaging them on their own terms and where they most like to interact.

The 10 steps towards constituents

The process for connecting to Internet constituents is relatively simple:

1. Identify the issue/topics relevant between the organization (industry sector or subject) and its perceived constituents (landscaping).
2. Identify existing active, aware, latent and non-publics (including, especially non-Internet publics) who are relevant to 1 above. This will require research into the places on the Internet where the issue is evident (Web sites, newsgroups, chat, etc) and what this audience knows and needs.
3. Identify what kind of Internet presence, content (richness), navigation, or intermediaries will be appropriate and, by assessing why you should have a Web site/Internet presence, what problems it will solve or what benefits can be derived.
4. From this you will be able to target the relevant properties or respond to the needs of visitors (to your Internet properties) and interested publics (at their preferred Internet properties or in their part of cyberspace).
5. Provide access to, collate and apply data, information and knowledge from within your organization to include in your Web site/Internet presence to meet the specific needs of your range of relevant constituents. This will be acquired from

internal publics, online and offline sources (and remember to look at corporate intranets and extranets).

6. With this knowledge, develop the creative concept and ask, 'Do I need to address different issues with different front pages/interaction for different publics?' This may mean that you will need to address stakeholder issues via a number of different types of Internet properties,. eg news media, newsgroups and pages on you own Web site/an alternative Web site.

7. Get the required Internet tools, skills and experience to develop the content and influence the relevant channel. This can be an in-house operation or bought in from qualified consultants.

8. Assess your concept or plan for effect on reputation arising from:
   - consequential porosity (information 'leaking out' of the organization);
   - consequential transparency (the information you deliberately expose about your organization); and
   - consequential agency (the way that the Internet constituents will change your messages and then expose their view to Internet opinion).

9. Assess the return on capital (eg is this extra transparency going to deliver cost-saving benefits, added value to internal stakeholders of corporate partners – you may have to go back to 1 above to access the greater benefit being revealed in this process now or in the future).

10. Trial the solution and test it to ensure that there are no 'bugs' in the system or other adverse effects on reputation or relationships.

Implement the programme

Of course, you will also monitor results, feedback and evaluate (eg achieved ROI, better service for less effort/cost/bigger or wider range of publics).

The development of such processes will identify the subject and issues, the medium for response and the means for engaging Internet constituents on their own terms.

FANS AND AMBASSADORS

Many organizations have amateur ambassadors. Many people have fans. These are people who collect memorabilia, histories, know-how and gossip and other information about organizations and famous people.

It will not be a surprise to know that they find other enthusiasts across the Internet. Sometimes this is in newsgroups and this enthusiasm is also often revealed in a Web site. In some sectors, such as sport, there is a significant online amateur industry devoted to players, teams and much more. Web sites are created by the score.

*** Over 500 Cameras now listed ***

Hi, and welcome to my growing collection of Kodak Cameras.

A few words about myself. I live in Jersey in the Channel Islands (Europe) and I look something like the self portrait

Figure 10.1 *An enthusiastic ambassador*

Ambassador properties, often completely funded and managed by individuals, can have a mass following with visitors running to millions. Some ambassador sites will have an amateur interest in your organization; others may have a commercial relationship. For example, shops, retailers, distributors, agents (The Prudential Insurance Company of America has hundreds of such sites), customers (car enthusiasts are an example) and many more of your Internet constituents are active on the Net. The practitioner who is landscaping and monitoring the Internet will find many Web sites that are suited to an ambassador programme.

AMBASSADOR SERVICES

www.dvisions.com

These sites offer a massive opportunity in a variety of directions. Of course, they will potentially drive traffic to your site and will offer significant third party endorsement. In addition, they offer added interest and understanding about the organization. They are less inhibited and frequently include information from many additional sources as well as a lot of personal experience.

Your organization may have one site but it may have dozens or hundreds of ambassador sites. Frequently, their combined reach will attract many times more Internet constituents than your organization's site.

A feature of these sites is that they often use the intellectual properties taken from the organization's site, are cavalier with information (such as giving out the chief executive's e-mail address) and can be quite emotional about events that affect the organization. That they may misrepresent your organization and even invent 'facts' is not unheard of and can give the practitioner a difficult issue to manage.

A relationship with these enthusiasts is inevitable at some time or another and thinking through what such relationships will or can be is better done sooner than later. Finding and considering what action you need to take is a big area for PR professionals.

There is no question that your organization should be proactive in identifying ambassador and fan sites and should have a sensitive strategy to develop effective relationships. Before you attempt to build a direct relationship with a fan site or an ambassador site or other Internet presence, you must review them in some detail (see Chapter 8). These sites have unilaterally claimed an allegiance with your organization and you will want to examine them in an effort to build effective (and commercially helpful) relationships. Each site is individual and must be treated as a one-off opportunity. However, there are some basic rules that can be applied to all:

- Go through opportunities and consequences (will one course of action create another opportunity, alert a wider public, give credibility to the site owner, widen interest?)
- Identify the opportunities for enhanced transparency and give the site more information – transparency. A football club might stream commentary during matches or interviews with players, etc.
- Elevate the quality of the site by offering trademarked logos, film clips, branded smiles, etc.
- Is an action going to box you in? Will other ambassador sites expect the same benefits?
- If the site gets very popular will you have to consider buying it?
- Are there ways you can devote limited resources to response but keep extra resources in reserve?
- Can you divide your response and engage the site in different ways (engage the site's constituents in another ways, offer added value third party resources)?
- Gauge your response and timing to offer development when the owner has the time and inclination.
- Wean the site owner off difficult practices (like copyright infringements) but always suggest, don't demand and always offer an added advantage as well.
- Where the site is blatantly infringing your intellectual property rights, turn the disadvantage into an advantage. Warner Brothers even offered free clips of their films to ambassadors with free Web site hosting to encourage people to show off their valuable intellectual property and turned what on the face of it was originally theft of copyright into a (very beneficial) ambassador programme.

Now you have the information you need to act.

Make sure you have a planned response and be prepared to be flexible. Use appropriate and ready-made processes and ensure that you can respond from a number of angles and through a variety of channels if needed. Use expertise, the strengths of your organization and the facilities of the Internet to aid your cause.

SPONSORSHIP

There is another form of third party site, which can be a powerful ambassador, and this is where your organization offers sponsorships.

Internet sponsorship works in many directions, at many levels and in a variety of ways. An organization may offer a range of Internet skills, information and intellectual property, Internet resources (eg hosting), banners, affiliate programmes or even financial support to other Internet properties. Offering these facilities will, as for all sponsorship, take time and will cost money. However, one of the advantages of Internet sponsorship is that much of the activity can often be automated and the cost versus the return can be advantageous.

There exists a form of so-called sponsorship that is evident on the Internet but which is, in reality, banner advertising. This is where a site owner places a banner advertisement on a Web page and encourages visitors to click on it, thereby taking their visitor to the site of the advertiser.

While the principle of creating opportunities for sites to offer 'click through' (paid for or not) has significant merit, the concept of sponsorship can go much further to the advantage of both properties. For many ambassador sites, the rewards can be no more that recognition, copyright images and easily available, but special advantages.

Internet skills

Many constituency organizations would like a Web site or would like to enhance their site. Some commercial and many voluntary and community Web sites are run on a shoestring or by volunteers. In many instances, there is a lack of skills, which offers an organization opportunities to both fill the skill gap and to help by teaching Internet techniques to enthusiastic amateurs or less than keen small businesses.

Such skills can extend to security advice and implementation, development of 'back office' processes such as online membership management, and even a credit card transaction service. To be able to offer such help to third parties is an extension of your corporate community programme.

Internet resources and facilities

Many portals and commercial Internet service providers already offer facilities such as free hosting and e-mail. Organizations can offer similar facilities but can go much further. There are some simple and inexpensive opportunities such as registering domain names, access to faster connections (ADSL, ISDN, etc) as well as hosting, security services and trading capability. For many voluntary organizations, a reasonable computer and modem may be relevant, or even Web software.

Intellectual properties

Your organization may be able to help by offering intellectual resources.

Warner Brothers provides hosting services and also offer clips of their films and music which enthusiasts can add to their sites for free. In the process, Warner Brothers have built a massive and enthusiastic following, with hundreds of amateur and voluntary sites using these facilities. But there may be simple things that can make a big difference, such as photographs, maps, drawings, software, etc. Many of the automated functions and Web facilities that your organization may take for granted can be rocket science or far too difficult or expensive for a small voluntary or charity site.

Banners

Many organizations pay site owners to include banner advertisements on their sites. For voluntary organizations these can become a revenue stream and help pay for their online presence. In addition they can reinforce the link between your organization and the site you are sponsoring. Being selective about such arrangements is important not only commercially (some commercial arrangements are not helpful) but in terms of the effect on reputation.

Affiliate programmes

If you sell using the Internet you can reward other sites (affiliates) for directing their visitors to your site. If when they arrive they carry out a desired action such as buying something from your site, you pay a reward to the affiliate. The 'payment' may be money but can easily be information, including intellectual property. There is a growing number of these arrangements and some companies provide the full managed service. The hard part is in finding appropriate online partners.

Creating such relationships with voluntary and charity groups can offer them revenues and as well as providing your organization with effective Internet visitors.

So far, we have seen how to build knowledge, identify media, create relevant messages and find distribution partners. Now we need to look at the process for presenting information to Internet constituents.

11

Reaching constituents with Web sites

We now have the principles we need to develop presence that should appeal to Internet constituents. The preparation, planning and development of content and application through different channels may take you to the point where you will want to create one or more Web sites.

Many practitioners work for organizations where the Web site is run and maintained by other parts of the organization. This does not diminish your responsibility for taking a very close interest in how it is constructed, who its visitors are and what it is achieving. At the end of the day, it represents a very powerful link between your organization and all your publics. It is, for most of your publics, stakeholders, constituents – call them what you will – the first point of contact. If your site does not come up to the mark, you, as a PR practitioner, have a professional responsibility to speak out and act.

FIRST THOUGHTS

Why should PR practitioners know about building a Web site?

The IT experts in a company are ideally suited to learning about HyperText Markup Language. The marketing department is adept at market segmentation and product differentiation. The advertising department is well tuned to above and below the line promotions, media buying and creative design. And so the arguments might continue.

But wait. Would the board put the IT department in charge of communicating? Is the marketing department trained in corporate affairs and is the advertising department ideal for one-to-one communication? The one department that is used to all these facets of corporate relationships (and many more) is PR. There are a host of other, relevant reasons but the most compelling is that an Internet presence creates a relationship with much more than a single or even a group of stakeholders. It provides a window for every form of interested party whether actively interested, dormant, just looking or potential Internet user.

Sure, the technology associated with the Internet needs IT input, the Web site needs information about products and services from marketers, and advertising is great for creating mass awareness; they are all valuable skills. The wide brief of relationship marketing is too stretched to take part in the societal and cultural exchange of corporate relationships where giving and receiving information and knowledge as well as experiences have much to do with empathy and little to do with the exchange of goods for money.

Web sites, because they offer relationships with constituents, are the responsibility of the department that is dedicated to relationship management and reputation. This is relationship management – the practice of PR in the raw. Web sites are very important to PR practice. Practitioners who do not know what content they must have, the constituents' agendas they must address and the impact they have on organizations, are falling behind in the ever-evolving skill sets that all of us must develop to be effective in the modern world.

This book does not show you how to build a Web site. There are lots of very good resources that offer such information. There is much necessary research and continuing development well beyond the scope of this book. This is not to say that practitioners should not learn how to create Web sites. An investment in a two-day course and a few winter evenings creating one's own site will be very instructive. Every practitioner will need to create Web pages and will need to learn how to upload them to a server. Learning how to do this before it is a forced process against a deadline is a very good idea. There is no reason why an intelligent and seasoned communicator cannot learn in a day what most 14-year-olds learn in a week.

While it may be fashionable to have a Web site (or several), there still is a case for taking at least one deep breath before contemplating whether to build one. To begin with, the very hour your Web site goes live, so will a further 20. Why should yours be so important? Then there are the managers who still doubt the need and someone who will want justification in a 10,000-word essay and it is all a terrible trial for too little tangible benefit. Be brave. Build your site and create resources to have an online presence. The payback will be great.

Corporate objectives

To be sure you want to build a site, examine your objectives for wanting it for communication. Such objectives will include what is to be achieved, how it will be measured and when project milestones will be achieved.

Measuring enhancements to relationships that meet corporate needs (such as provision of information, creating empathy to sell or provide services, products, entertainment or knowledge) within an agreed timescale are commonly used objectives. Such considerations may have very commercial objectives such as cost reduction for online (or offline) sales.

As for all activities – Internet or otherwise – there are two ways of looking at investment. Adding £10,000 of turnover may deliver £2,000 profit to the bottom line (at 20 per cent return on investment in a year). Cutting £1,000 off costs will deliver £1,000 profit to the bottom line. Is your Web site going to increase turnover or reduce costs or are there other objectives? Are they well developed before you go so far as to spend so much effort and money?

Build relationships

Once the corporate objective is clear, the decision to implement a

Web site can only be to build and sustain a relationship with constituents via the Internet. These relationships will recognize that the site visitors choose to open the opportunity for the relationship. The organization, at best, can only invite a relationship and then work very hard at sustaining it.

Provide access

Your organization is providing access to a lot of information. It will be available to a wide constituency. Relationships and reputation are exposed all the time. Your site is an online view of your organization's public relations all the time and all over the world. Access is enriched through an understanding of the relationship between the corporate objectives and online constituents' association with them. By watching what interests visitors (through analysis of site visit records) you can identify interest in types of pages and how that chimes with the core messages you believe may interest your constituents. This may lead to a reappraisal of the site, your objectives or even the corporate aims and ambitions. In addition, you may engage constituents by interacting with them (but only with their consent and permission).

In addition to, or separate from the corporate Web site, there may be other good reasons to develop Web pages.

One or more Web sites?

In many cases organizations have corporate Web sites. These sites can be very comprehensive and offer significant information for a very broad as well as for select constituents.

One of the most important reasons for site development is to be able to distinguish the elements of corporate brand equity or to differentiate between corporate assets. In other words, what is special about your organization and what is its special knowledge, facility or thing. For example, a company that manufactures many brands such as household products, cars or beverages, may want a Web presence for each brand, product series or type of drink.

Some organizations have a product or process that is applicable to disparate consumers or applications. This may mean that a Web site has to address the needs of each consumer group in terms relevant to their interest rather than trying to design an all-purpose site. For example, a button manufacturer may want to sell buttons to home dressmakers, fashion houses and clothing manufacturers. Each will have different information and supply needs, such as the range and delivery by post, or next year's range and samples delivered by courier, or machine-friendly features and volume delivery in a van. Each type of consumer would find information for the other irrelevant.

There is a great case for looking at your Web presence from many angles. You may want to offer a range of experiences or to explore different themes and approaches in your Internet presence. It is not an either/or choice because you can have them all. Many organizations have different sites for different things, events, activities, products, brands or just for this month's departmental outing.

It is not just companies that need to make these decisions. Government departments may like to distinguish between, say, the Valuation Office and its parent organization, Her Majesty's Inland Revenue Service. Of course, there should be a process by which the Web site visitor can identify the relationship. If this is not apparent (and navigation simple) then the Internet visitor is likely to doubt the relationship or the nature of the relationship and whether the site can be trusted.

As for a company or government department, so too for a charity, political party and even a family's own Web site. Thus, there are considerations for aiming a site at vertical markets or interests and horizontal information seekers.

Visitor-centric relationships

Because Internet relationships are very personal, the visitor will look at the site to meet a number of self-centric needs.

A potential customer may be from a business with budgets running to millions of pounds, or a private citizen. The nature of the Internet is such that, because an individual (whether a corporate buyer or private citizen) has significant choice from multiple vendors, many factors come into play.

Every study of motivation for using the Internet shows users have an interest in the range and variety of information. Most users are disappointed when their activity comes to a dead end. Many back out of such sites never to return. The site is a gateway to nowhere! A cul-de-sac, a blockage in the user's progress through cyberspace, is not an appealing prospect. On the other hand, a site that is a gateway to rich and endless interest and excitement is always worth revisiting.

Creating a site that is appealing to dwell in is an excellent aim, but there is a very good case for creating an elegant and enriching form of escape. The average visitor to a theme park will stay for about five hours. The reason is that, at the end of that time, the park operator knows that they will be tired and only spend marginally more money, and if they go on all the rides, there will be no incentive to return. The theme park operators will go to extraordinary lengths to entertain people in queues for rides, will provide vended services at strategic locations and reward people for staying until they have a little money left and some rides yet to experience. Then, without the visitor noticing how, they are gently encouraged to leave.

A good Web site will know when it has done enough and it is time to send the visitor on his or her way, vowing to return soon.

PR CONSIDERATIONS FOR WEB SITE CONTENT

Basic requirements

There is lots of research that tells us about what you have to do when designing and putting up a Web site. For the PR practitioner, this is a double-edged sword. There is often considerable urgency (with the potential to take short cuts) and there is an absolute imperative for maintaining trust.

The credibility of the practitioner recommending that a Web site should be created and that a site can and will conform to basic principles is critical. Practitioners must ensure that their promise (and that of their organization) to Internet constituents includes assurances and performance that it is:

- secure;
- trustworthy;
- convenient;
- private;
- fast;
- fresh.

AWESOME POWER IN SECONDS

People do not like to think they are being exposed to the awesome power of the Internet, and fear it. At the same time they are impatient to get to the information and experience they hoped for. JoAnna Brandi (http://www.customerretention.com) likes to epitomize this particular cultural trait as surfing while muttering, 'Come on, come on, I don't have all minute!'. This means that download times, navigation and concise and accurate information are critical.

Corporate and product brand equity brings with it a sense of trust and comfort.

In the Internet world, where brands are presented to global constituents, brand equity in one country may be completely absent in another. In addition, the Internet has spawned a lot of new organizations. Why should any Internet site be trusted?

Our constituents want to deal with organizations that can be trusted: companies that promise to protect their customers' interests, government departments that speak in plain understandable language, universities that explain what they do, e-zines that have trustworthy journalists and above all organizations that meet their promises.

Online consumers want assurances that products will live up to the specifications and that the colours will match what they see on the screen. They want a solemn undertaking that credit card information is safe. They need assurance that buying habits will not be used to second-guess what you may feel they might what. More than that, they want to be sure that their details and information will not be posted on to other organizations and their lifestyle sold to the highest bidder for who knows what purpose.

This means that the site and what it offers has to demonstrate that its use is safe, trustworthy and private. These are the promises you must hold out and the values you must adhere to. These are characteristics that are earned, and cannot be implied or glossed over. There is no flashy site graphic that will substitute for the fundamental fidelity of a Web site.

The issue of security and trust highlights the much publicized attacks on sites. They happen all the time (for examples see:

http://www.attrition.org/). While site security is essential, so too is your issues management programme for when, despite all your precautions, site integrity is breached. It will happen to you. You must have issues management processes in place and they must be rehearsed (we cover this subject in Chapter 17). It just means sticking to old values like integrity and trustworthiness, which is not always easy when faced with the organization's needs for speed and constituents' requirements for convenience.

Internet users want to make decisions and move on. Time spent on the Internet is 'raiding' time that could be spent doing something else. A consumer made to pause to reconsider may go elsewhere.

FRESH ALL THE TIME

'A fresh site says all kinds of positive things,' says Andy Howarth, president of Snickelways Interactive, a New York-based development firm. 'The message is "we care about you, we're up to date, we know what's going on". But if you don't keep your site fresh, the message is "we're boring, we don't know what we're doing, and we don't care".'[1]

- weigh the costs and benefits of daily, weekly, monthly or quarterly infusions of new content;
- decide who is responsible for updates;
- determine what updating must be done manually and what can be automated;
- find out if there is software that can make updating easy for the non-programmers in your organization;
- create a schedule for maintaining the site and stick to it;
- tell your site users how up to date your information is.

DEFINING CONTENT
Products, services and marketing

Adding a product or service to a Web site may also mean the prac-

---

[1] Howarth, A quoted in *Admedium Newsletter*; January 1998

titioner has to define information that prospective visitors may need. This may include all or a mix and match of the following:

- product specification (design, functionality, expertise, etc);
- delivery;
- how easy it is to do business with the company;
- how the processes of purchase are managed;
- how the processes of delivery are managed;
- how the processes for payment are managed;
- the nature of guarantees and warranties;
- how after-sales care is managed;
- the returns policy and how it is managed;
- communication, especially when things go wrong (and global interaction means time shifting).

Even when these considerations are the responsibility of another department, the execution of your online capability is a major reputation issue. If your organization cannot perform, you will need to build bridges with consumers fast and effectively.

There is often a case for developing content for wider audiences in this part of your Web site. Information about design, processes and resources (drawings, cartoons, factory layouts) can engage constituents, nearby communities or local government.

Societal issues

For marketing purposes the considerations outlined above may be quite sufficient, but for the Internet constituent they may be very wide of the mark. With opinion polls showing the influence of ethical purchasing gaining ground by the day, there are wider considerations.

Does the relationship with your organization chime with the same ethical, environmental or other considerations of the visitor? The questions in the visitors' mind may include the organization's structures and beliefs. Those components that are associated with the social contract can be greater than a commercial or legal framework for your site visitor and may need to be considered in framing the Web site brief.

People seek a trustworthy relationship. Elements of this social contract fall into three categories: fidelity, employee and external stakeholder consideration. The extent to which an organization wishes or needs to create transparency about its activities will vary but can be one or a combination of the following models.

The organization's fidelity

An audience with an interest in fidelity will have specific interests in some key elements as part of his or her relationship with the organization.

What is important to note is that we can now begin to see some very broad subjects becoming quite specific in nature. This specificity is important. The culture of the organization is broad and is evident in many contexts. These subjects are quite complex and may have the elements shown in Figure 11.1. Most companies would need to be able to identify these contexts in order to be able to manage questions about their culture.

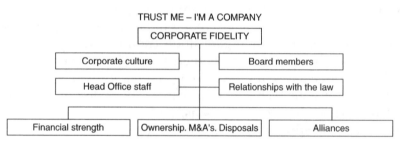

Figure 11.1 *Fidelity may have a place on your Web site*

Some board members have a significant influence on the reputation of companies. A manager like Richard Branson offers a lot to the reputation and the relationships of the Virgin companies. Managers in some other organizations have a less beneficial impact which has led to a huge online industry looking for and 'exposing' so-called 'fat cats'. The Internet constituency is quite capable of finding such information from a number of Internet third parties. Such issues may need to be addressed as part of the content of the Web site. Alternatively, they may be addressed in a different and separate, but probably hyperlinked, Web site.

If your organization does not present its case, who will fill the gap and would you appreciate the content they may use?

When looking for messages in the public domain it is helpful to examine which ones are affecting the reputation of an organization.

A capability to survive

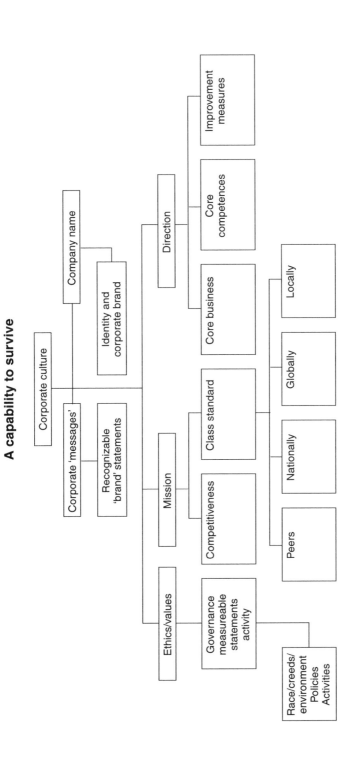

Figure 11.2 *Are Internet constituents interested in management capability?*

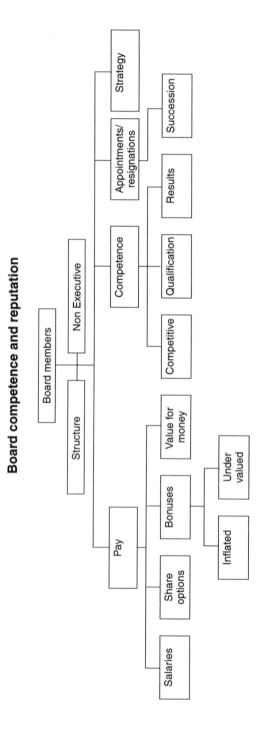

Figure 11.3 *Do Internet constituents have an interest in board behaviour?*

Reputed for financial stability

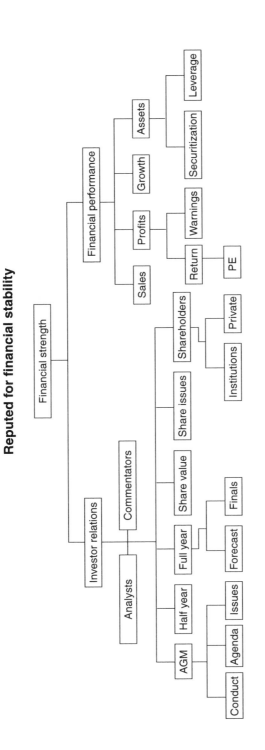

Figure 11.4 *A reputation for being financially sound*

Perceptions about managers in the City and among customers may be completely at odds with each other. Because of the transparency afforded by information across the Internet all audiences have access to a mass of information about most corporate managers.

Corporate fidelity may be seen more clearly in terms of financial performance and investor relations. A company without the ability to raise money from investors, make profits and grow, has a real reputation problem. The very foundation of many transactions is based on fiscal trust. Will the company survive and continue to offer benefits to customers, investors, employees, suppliers and many other stakeholders? The Web audience may want answers to such questions.

Measuring the fidelity of a company in terms of its financial reputation is a very helpful process. Most people do it when they make decisions about organizations. The messages that describe financial performance are richly reported. Knowing what they are, watching out for them and collating the results, is often done simply based on an article or an analyst's newsletter. Using a structured process and analysis across a range of reports and media, a more rounded view can be identified.

The same applies to the acquisitive nature of some companies and the vulnerabilities of others. Ownership of companies and the mass of speculation about mergers and acquisitions can be structured to offer comfort to the site visitor and monitoring can provide early warning of much of this activity. Issues of ownership may be expressed in the way shown in Figure 11.5.

As with most events, there are very few surprises if relevant attention can be paid to a wide enough range of opinions. Although managers tend to be aware of their opportunities and vulnerabilities, the depth of conjecture is frequently more important than mere presence.

Employees

One of the key points made by the Public Relations Internet Commission is the nature and growing significance of porosity, the extent to which information 'leaks' out of organizations and is available to the global Internet constituency.

As more companies buy in services, many people who were once employees find themselves contractors. Of those who remain

A question of ownership

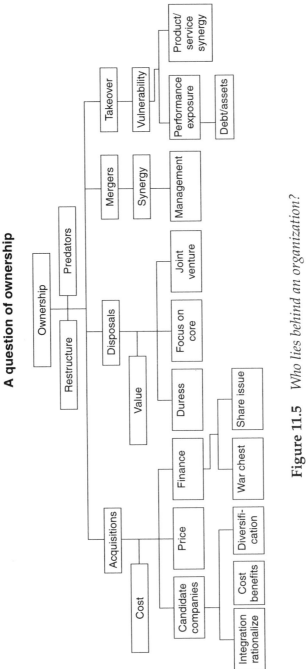

Figure 11.5 *Who lies behind an organization?*

employed, a new relationship has evolved. Employees are often stakeholders in a variety of ways. They can also be shareholders, local community leaders and pressure group activists. As such, the internal and external messages have a range and context that have grown and will continue to grow. This can be expressed in a series of messages expressed on the subjects shown in Figure 11.6.

Corporate citizen

Directors are spending more time looking beyond their companies. Part of this is because the global market is becoming more apparent at every level of operation and partly because there are many institutions that can, quite quickly, have a mighty impact.

The number of industry regulators, government administrators, pressure groups and community interests is astonishing. There are over 300 recognizable activist groups with an Internet presence in the UK.

The context shown in Figure 11.7 gives some clue as to the messages that are derived from beyond the company but are significant to its growth and prosperity.

For each of such groupings there are key messages, and this should be the concern of every manager. For most companies the messages already exist, reflecting the nature and evolution of the organization. However, there are many means to ensure that the appropriate messages are effectively audited: content analysis of media and company literature is one example.

E-PUBS

There are many variants of Web sites (millions of them) and inventing your own online 'newspaper' – e-pub – has become fashionable.

E-pubs act as the equivalent of a company newsletter, magazine or newspaper. The target publics for the traditional printed versions could include employees, dealers, distributors, retailers, analysts, shareholders, suppliers and even local communities. Today, some of these publics can take advantage of Internet interconnectivity to access information. You can make it more current and the delays in delivery and distribution are minimized.

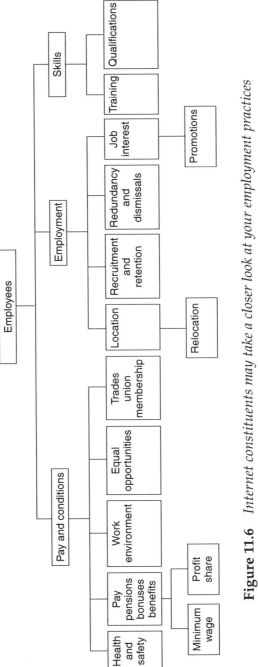

Figure 11.6 *Internet constituents may take a closer look at your employment practices*

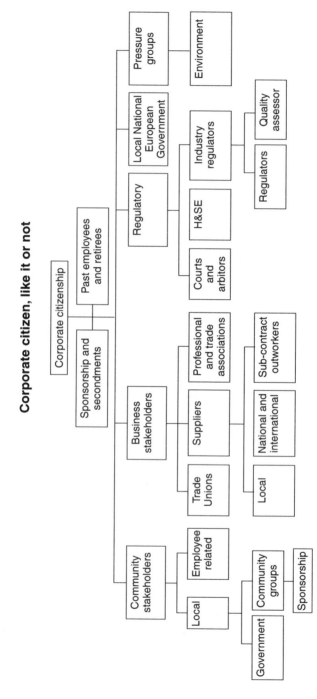

Figure 11.7 *How your organization relates to its external stakeholders, local citizens, or even governments may be important for your site*

There is a case for identifying whether your organization needs to use both online and offline corporate publications – not everyone is happy with online reading. There are opportunities to amalgamate online and offline production by arranging for small batch, on location or contracted remote printing and distribution. This is done by sending the page production direct to the printing facility from your extranet (to a printer or, in some cases, direct to a photocopier at a remote location).

E-PUB THINGS TO THINK ABOUT

- objective;
- frequency;
- who will be responsible (editor);
- budget;
- building the list of Internet constituents who will receive your e-pub;
- designing the online (and, as appropriate, offline version);
- content development;
- identifying sources for information/copy;
- copywriting;
- editing;
- secondary or tertiary applications for content (and added value);
- return on investment.

E-pubs can include supplements such as safety and quality assurance information and much of the paperwork many companies send to employees and other stakeholders. Using the Internet can save a small fortune in print costs.

WEBCASTING

Webcasting is still in its infancy but as more people have access to ADSL, ISDN and interactive television and other broadband facilities, this form of communication will become progressively more significant both for business use and for communicating with

Internet constituents. The reason is simple: Webcasts will deliver full colour moving pictures with sound and simultaneous interactivity with a lot of other content and facilities. That is for the future and expectations are high, but it does highlight the need for Internet PR to judiciously begin to use this medium.

Applications for Webcast include a virtual press conference, product presentation, lecture, annual reports, product launches and issues management. By logging on to a Web address, a journalist in New York or reporter in Delhi can receive a movie and interact with the person making the Webcast. As Interactive Television (iTV) becomes more significant, news desks will want to be able to offer movie options to television viewers and will be desperately short of resources. In fact anything where moving visual impact, face-to-face communication and interactivity is needed offers resource for the publisher and exposure opportunities for the organization.

The benefits of reduced travel costs, personal interactivity, added content and background information as well as involvement are well understood. In addition, Webcast can be made available like a TV broadcast (see http://www.bbc.co.uk/audiovideo/).

Some warnings:

- It is very easy to make Webcasts dull and boring.
- Without excellent connections the sound and vision can be out of sync, and there may be delays in transmission.
- Facilities for Webcasting can be quite basic or very sophisticated. The essential consideration is to combine the facilities of a television broadcast (camera, lighting, sound, editing, etc), and interactive content.
- Webcast is streamed information. This means that the flow of data is continuous and it takes up a lot of transmission resource (bandwidth). For this reason your recipient will need fast access (minimum 56k) and be able to access your Webcast through a firewall (if one exists), which tend to restrict file size or bandwidth use. Using Webcast is not good at the time of going to press unless both parties have good bandwidth. This is getting better all the time and ADSL will make a big difference to millions of PC Internet users in the UK.
- The platform you use is significant. Some people receive infor-

mation using RealPlayer, others use AVI (Windows Media Player) or other programs. You may need to offer a facility to download the player of your choice or broadcast using both (or more) systems.

- Paying attention to how your Webcast will appear at the receiver's end is all-important and trialling with perhaps pre-broadcast liaison is essential. Do a test run to ensure that the Webcast is acceptable at the other end and that it can be interactive.
- You may have to guide your receiver/their IT department in how to set up their browser and their video reception software.

There is every good reason to evaluate Webcasts to see how effective they are as an aid to learning and improving capability.

VNRs on the Web

It is very unpopular these days to call a Video News Release (VNR) by its name, but video clips are created by companies for use by broadcasters.

The virtual press office may offer a range of formats to help journalists view clips to make decisions as to whether they want to use any of your footage. However, downloading high-quality (television broadcast) video images has to be a professional job. The available clips will need to have been shot using broadcast quality equipment and tape and will need to be professionally edited. In addition, its transmission will need to be by ISDNx2 (120kbs) or faster, using T1 connections.

There are alternatives including professional companies that can shoot, edit and create pages for your Web site, designed for online viewing by TV editors and those who host the big video files, ready to transmit to the TV station. The pages can be hosted, edited and managed by the contractor but will look as though they are on your Web site in your virtual press office. Much the same advice applies for sound clips.

The reason sound and video are now so much more important is the reach you have via the organization's Web site. Broadcasters round the world may want to use your material and, in this content-hungry era, there are hundreds of outlets available when only a few years ago there were but a handful.

SITE DEVELOPMENT AND MAINTENANCE

Having identified the strategic reasons and identified the need to consider reputation issues, content and a lot more, the processes for creating a site and its development will proceed and will include the following elements.

Content design

A Web site needs to communicate with the online audience in a manner that effectively utilizes the interactive nature of the medium. Content has to be accurate, compelling and to the point.

There should be useful online resources that will encourage repeat Web site traffic.

Graphic design

Web site visitors will measure an organization's professionalism and sophistication by the impression they get during the first few (say, 15) seconds they spend on its Web site. Designing a professional and consistent look and feel for a Web site is critical to its acceptance. There is a need to provide an engaging graphic design while respecting the unique set of constraints caused by the limitations of the computer screen resolution and the slow connection speeds of many users.

Architectural design

Making a Web site easy to navigate and presenting information in an intuitive, comprehensible and comfortable layout are the core of the architectural design of a Web site. Architectural design should help guide the viewer along a path that effectively presents the desired message.

Testing

Web site testing is used to evaluate the site's performance for a variety of user configurations and browsers, and to gauge its effectiveness with trial audiences. There is no way of saying how important site testing is. Before a site goes public it must be tested. Its security must be bullet proof. It has to be checked from every angle. Does its interactivity work? If a visitor sends an e-mail from your site does it prompt an immediate and relationship-enhancing response? Is the whole thing scaleable? If you get 10 or 10 million hits, what strategy is in place to meet visitor needs?

The experience of companies like the Halifax, Barclays Bank and Powergen are all very good examples of how, when the Web site fails, we all find out about it! Publicists were culpable when their dotcom investment broker clients' reputations were damaged through promotion that overwhelmed the back offices, which could not cope with demand.

The PR practitioner needs to be paranoid about testing.

Maintenance

Unlike a printed brochure, a Web site is an evolving communication. In addition, the site has to be kept fresh. The Internet constituent may visit a site more frequently than a favourite retail outlet. A month-old Web site can seem like last winter's shop window.

In addition, hyperlinks and links between pages on a site become dated very quickly and do not work. There is software to help monitor your (and anyone else's) site.

You may also want to monitor how your site ranks among search engines.

Domain names

Domain names started out to help computers connect through the Internet and have now become, among other things, the way we know companies and organizations, like Amazon.com. This has given rise to cybersquatting disputes (someone registering your organization's name in an attempt to sell it back to you), which reflects the premium that businesses are placing on domain names and their potential for electronic commerce.

With the growth of the Internet, domain names have increasingly come into conflict with trademarks. Trademarks are administered by public authorities and give rights to trademark holders. Domain names are usually administered by non-governmental organizations on a first-come, first-served basis and are a global presence on the Internet. Cybersquatters exploit the differences in the two systems by taking advantage of the less formalized nature of the domain names system. Recent international cooperation has begun to create some order out of this chaos but there is some way to go.

A group of countries (Australia, Argentina, Canada, Denmark, European Union, France, and the United States) are promoting the protection of intellectual property rights and domain names. Such issues include abusive registrations of trade names, geographical indications and other rights not based on trademarks. There is likely to be a WIPO (World Intellectual Property Organization) proposal on best practices and conventions to help administrators of country code top level domain name registries to prevent and resolve domain names disputes.

As one might expect, the Internet does not stand still and now there is the opportunity to create longer domain names that are similar to complete sentences; an example might be http://www.InternetPublicRelations.co.uk. The opportunities seem like a lot of fun for creative PR practitioners. In the mean-time, they need to be aware of their legal responsibilities and should act within the law and in good faith.

Other site-building considerations

Setting up domain name services and Web site hosting can be undertaken by the organization or can be contracted out. Domain names should always be owned by the organization and regis-tering names and their likeness across the world is a necessary precaution against cybersquatting.

Make sure adequate bandwidth and server capacity are avail-able to handle the load of the Web site. All too often the ability to cope with Web site traffic brings an organization's reputation into disrepute. There are precautions that can be taken and an ability to add capacity at short notice must be considered. You may also want to keep a mirror site available.

Further things to consider include:

- Maintaining adequate security of the server and any data collected over the Web site. This is not a 'nice to have' option. It is essential.
- The need to implement advanced features such as CGI, Java and other programming to enable sophisticated interactivity and special Web site features.

- Collecting and processing the Web site access log and user-provided data to gain a comprehensive understanding of traffic patterns within the Web site itself and into the Web site from external sources. Don't collect information – use it.
- Information provided by users of the Web site kept as databases has to be registered under the provisions of the Data Protection Act; make sure you comply.
- Ensure you have adequate and comprehensive security systems when building interfaces that allow Web site users to access the organization's databases.
- Installing search engines on to Web sites to facilitate access to large volumes of information.
- Providing ancillary services such as electronic mailing lists (listserv), autoresponders, FTP service (to allow files to be downloaded), and e-mail forwarding. This is needed to ensure that the organization is capable of interacting with visitors and is an aid to visitors' interest and retention.

PROMOTING YOUR WEB SITE

The many ways for promoting a Web site identified in this book extend well beyond the traditional forms of promotion.

The basics are well documented elsewhere and require little comment here. The importance of ensuring that all stationery, brochures, advertisements and applications of corporate identity includes the Web site address does not need much more emphasis. Failure to ensure such basics are adhered to is simply negligent and ranks alongside not including a telephone number on your Web site or visiting cards.

Above and below the line advertising and PR is now much in use and has offered the publicists excellent revenue streams for several years. The newer forms of online promotion, including e-mail, banner advertising, affiliate promotion, are also well documented and where they have a PR role, particularly affecting relationships and reputation, they are covered in this book.

There are two aspects of online marketing that require closer attention. Search engines are important because of their growing significance as an aid to knowledge management. In addition, they have become a valuable aid in identification of online relationships and relevance of Web sites and Internet comment to companies, brands and issues. Linking between sites is very relevant because of the implied endorsements such activities bring with them. Customer relationship marketing (CRM) is also very significant. This is true, not so much for current applications, but for the future impact one-to-one relationships will have as the Internet matures. CRM goes beyond Web site development and is dealt with in Chapter 15.

Search engines

Because search engines are the primary way most people find Web sites, it is relevant to know how to add your site to an engine and what needs to be done to optimize your efforts. Nearly every Web site builder will have a view – and a promise. Few are expert and the competition is fierce.

There are many tools and tricks on the way to being at the top and there are people who specialize in this activity. They are called search engine optimization (SEO) specialists. It is sensible to have your SEO specialist close by you as you develop your site. It is much harder to restructure the site or re-enter information on Web page codes (HTML tags) after the event than during construction.

Web crawlers, the robots that seek out Web pages for search engines, look for key words on Web pages. They index the site by looking at the Web pages and match the content against the rules of the search engine. There is no point in having key words and key word phrases inside HTML tags without considering an overall online promotion strategy. It is helpful to use expertise to write for the search engines, analyse site statistics and to have a thorough knowledge of Web crawler-friendly words. In addition, it is important to stay up to date on search engine developments.

If your competitors regularly achieve higher ranking in search engine searches, there may be a temptation to examine their Meta tags (an easy process on most browsers – click view, then source and there it is) and find out what the secret is. 'Stealing Meta tags' is a common tactic. If the content of your page is stolen, then it is copyright infringement.

The real long-term advantage will come from a good Web site with pages that are easy to read. Give the search engines and your end-users a navigation scheme that they can easily follow. By giving your target audience exactly what they are searching for, you are also adding value to the search engines.

12

Reaching internal audiences

Most organizations have developed an intranet or have adapted a LAN as a tool to make information available online and help improve employee relations. Many organizations find their investment is not showing an effective return on investment.

Most companies' intranets do not reflect the external online (Web site) ethos of the company and immediately create an impression of 'them' outside the organization and 'us' inside the organization.

The theory of an intranet is that it allows every employee to possess that same knowledge as every other employee and with a few clicks, an employee can tap into research, background information, case studies, his or her personal file, pay rates, holiday entitlement, a biographical note on the chairman and much more. Most intranets are not like this at all. They have masses of inaccessible information, are seldom integrated with work patterns and they have convoluted firewalls that make the Great Wall of China look like a bedroom curtain. This is the response by an IT department to meet the paranoia of managers who have suddenly been exposed to the prospect that they and their department may be transparently accountable.

The truth is that most managers are unaware of the amount of information that is already in the public domain, that their organization is perfectly transparent and, worse, porous to the point of embarrassment. Furthermore, where the public has little information, the nature of Internet agency invents what is unknown.

Many intranets spawn a culture where employees find ways of circumnavigating firewalls. It becomes a habit and as a result, truly valuable information becomes almost impossible to protect and accessibility progressively more difficult. It is much better to have a few important firewalls and a culture that believes they are essential and a good thing for security, than one where employees buck the system. To misquote George Orwell, 'Firewalls bad... security culture good'.

Simple navigation conventions are an overriding consideration. They should reflect the navigation conventions for Web visitors, suppliers and virtual partners. They should be an aid to e-enablement and the culture of working in an information-rich world.

All employees should be able to create their own pages. They should be able to configure (and reconfigure) them for individual purpose. The concept that employees should add data because there is an intrinsic value to their role and self-esteem should prevail. Why should the HR department need to enter data about an employee's change of address? There is no reason on earth other than it is part of the job description. There is every reason why an employee should if that is where the pay cheque notification is delivered. What is more the data will be accurate and up to date! Other examples include expense reports and time sheets; holiday entitlement, pension and share option contributions will add interest too.

INTRANETS NEED TO BE FUN TOO

As for any Web site, the integrity of an intranet has to obey the essential rules of being:

- secure, so that employees can use it with confidence;
- trustworthy, so that employees do not feel threatened by it;
- convenient, as a contribution to enhanced working;

- private, so that it can be used for internal inter-departmental interactivity'
- fast, to save time, make content accessible and to aid productivity;
- fresh so that information is up to date;
- involving.

Simple, standardized methods for adding information are a must. In this way, knowledge management is simplified and easy to accomplish.

There are some very simple aids that will add to the value of an intranet: a dictionary, acronym buster, corporate (and personal) address book, integrated e-mail, buddy list, instant messaging, discussion lists, and project management programmes. Virtual safety, training and education content are helpful too. The virtual in-house newspaper, employees' mart, and departmental news are all part of the deal.

External access to the richness of the Internet is essential for an organization to be competitive. It is after all the biggest library in the world. The ability to use recognized evaluation tools to assess reliability and add important sites to the corporate store of knowledge is essential. Access to the corporate catalogue of information (including properly evaluated external data) should be available both as a catalogue and via a search engine but above everything else, should be standard. Employees, like any other Internet constituent, will refer to an intranet several times a day if it affects them personally and is an aid to their work.

All too often, organizations are afraid of abuse. For the most part, this is a question of lack of knowledge. Employees have a vested interest in protecting their own good name and that of the company. Knowing the opportunities for damage to their own and their colleagues' reputation and well-being, is one of the greatest motivations for security and responsible use. In addition, when the advantages of responsible use are obvious, the incentive to apply it sensibly becomes apparent. In addition, it should be the means by which added achievement becomes obvious in terms of reducing cost, enhanced interactivity, increasing throughput and faster times to market. Public goal setting and achievement made transparent via an intranet, enhance commitment. There will be abuse but there will be every incentive for achievement as considerable peer pressure focuses effort on attainment.

When the man at the factory gate can see over-budget and underperformance graphs for the marketing department, long lunches disappear. It is not that the gatekeeper was unaware before, that the rumours did not permeate the company or that external audiences did not know; these things have been known about through history. It is the fact that the information is transparent to all that really counts. It also adds another element, a driving need to be competitively better, because more competitor knowledge is available on the intranet as well!

The intranet has to obey the rules that apply to a Web site. Its content must be complete and rich, it has to reach throughout the organization, it needs to recognize the range of needs and interests of employee constituents and it must be responsive to their aspirations. It should also be fun.

13

Using e-mail for communication

E-mail communication brings out schizophrenia spots on most people. We receive mountains and have difficulty managing them. We like the speed and interactivity and like to be able to send information to a wide range of people easily and quickly. On the other hand e-mail is intrusive and if there is one thing we all dislike, its unsolicited mail – spam.

E-MAIL MARKETING

For issuing business information such as a press release it is great. When used properly, marketing via e-mail is brilliant. It offers a personal and personalized way of communicating directly with a customer.

Getting to know a journalist, colleague or customer, and then tailoring an offer specifically to suit his or her needs is the perfect form of electronic communication. However, if you set out to bombard people as part of a list with standard, unsolicited commercial e-mail, you will fail. People get angry when they receive spam. And they are angry with the people who send it.

The benefits

- E-mail marketing campaigns deliver directly to the recipient.
- It conveys your precise message.
- People respond directly to e-mails.
- It requires little effort on your part and on the part of the recipient.
- It's cheap.

Over the past few years, personalized e-mail campaigns have proven to have one of the highest returns on investment when used with discretion.

E-mail allows a company to distribute its messages in an assortment of ways and to customize many messages appropriate to the recipients' needs. It lends itself to mail merge for close message matching.

SPAM RESOURCE

There are facilities that allow you to identify and manage people and organizations that contact you or your site. You can find out a lot about people who spam sites and you can manage your relationship with them using these tools: http://samspade.org; Cyberkit; WS_Ping ProPack; and NetScanTools.

E-mail also allows for specific tracking of campaigns, as detailed and precise as knowing who has clicked through to your Web site; how many people have simply opened up the message and how many have forwarded it on to others?

On the downside

Bulk e-mail sent out without the user's permission and without his or her knowledge of what lies inside the message can alarm the recipient (especially when there are attachments).

Also, it's very easy to completely destroy you relationship with the recipient – forever.

E-MAIL RELATIONSHIPS

Today, e-mail is used for most commercial and personal exchanges of information and advertising, the complete sales cycle and to provide customer service and support. Each of the commercial contacts is an opportunity for your organization to enhance or harm your relationships and reputation. You have to be aware that e-mail is a very potent method for creating and sustaining corporate and product brands. Every e-mail contact has an effect on your brand.

The nature of your relationships (and that of your whole organization) will be reflected in your e-mail relationships. Tone in e-mails reflects on your image. The tone of the contact, whether polite, serious, formal, dry, business-like, light and friendly (overfriendly), reflects on the personality of the organization. Does your e-mail look like everybody is petrified of legal action?

Setting standards for your organization is helpful especially when the whole organization is aware of the opportunities and pitfalls. It is very easy to slip into assuming a relationship or to become too chatty on the basis of many e-mail exchanges. The truth is that e-mail is impersonal and provides little insight into the needs, aspirations and social background or interests of the person at the other end.

You will make decisions on the image you want to project, and will attempt to be consistent. In the same way and with the same consistency, this needs to be true of customer service people, production, accounts and purchasing people, indeed everyone with contact between your organization and those receiving its e-mails.

Responding to Web contacts using e-mail

Putting up a Web site is an open invitation to people to send you e-mail. How quickly you respond makes a huge impression.

Speed of response is very impressive, as long as the answer is well considered. The speed of response is a subject in itself. If it is a reply to a lost password query, immediacy is essential. If it is delayed, you will lose your contact because he or she will move on to some other task. If e-mail languishes unanswered within your organization, the possible reactions are that your e-mail doesn't work, your organization lacks capability to use e-mail, or that you are too busy and don't care.

An instant auto-response that bounces back telling your contact that the message was received isn't necessarily a positive brand experience either. Sometimes it suggests that this is a delaying tactic or that the sender is not important enough to get personal attention. Used effectively it may say the message was received and is being treated personally (by a real, knowledgeable, appropriate and interested person). It also has to say who responded – a point of contact if things go wrong.

Work with colleagues on the image you want your organization's information partners to have. Identify why and be careful to note the arguments. Ensure that effective, reasoned and personal tuition is available throughout the organization. It is important to explain how e-mails can disclose a lot about the organization, its culture and approach to its Internet constituents and the person using e-mail.

Internet mailing lists

A mailing to people who subscribe to a periodic mailing distribution on a particular topic is a popular way to keep up with what is of interest or professionally significant. Many software producers and other vendors use them as a way to keep in touch with customers. The e-groups list (http://groups.yahoo.com) is one of the most popular and allows PR people to subscribe to a range of relevant experts and colleagues with information of professional interest. There are thousands of mailing lists and many of them are available to the public.

A LIST SERVER

A list server is a software program designed to manage one or more mailing lists. One of the more popular packages is named 'Listserv'. Other popular packages include Listproc, Majordomo, Yahoo! Groups, and Mailserve. Most importantly not all mailing lists run on list servers: there are many that are manually managed and are moderated. Listserv, used to engage Internet constituents through distribution of knowledge, has considerable benefits including opportunities to include third party expertise.

It is easy to confuse a mailing list and a list server. A mailing list is a type of e-mail distribution in which e-mail is sent to a fixed site that holds a list of e-mail recipients and mail is then distributed to those recipients automatically (or through a moderator). Sometimes list server content is distributed immediately and sometimes only at specific times and in batches of e-mails, the principle being that a person or organization with expert of special information can distribute notes about it to members who have signed up to receive e-mails sent out using a list server.

Applications for the use of list servers are very wide. A list server is an excellent tool for product managers, account executives and experts. It is also used by people who aggregate information from online and offline resources, which saves members of the list serve group endless hours of surfing or reviewing Web pages.

This is a workaday tool that every PR person should have available and should use. Its application where individuals sign up to accept information is very powerful because the recipients have given permission to have information sent to them.

The key to the use of list servers is in always being relevant, having germane headings and recognizing that if the information is not relevant, people will just stop receiving your copy.

There is a list server related to this book, which can be found at: http://groups.yahoo.com/group/netreputation.

THE DANGERS OF SPAM

Unsolicited bulk e-mail

E-mail with substantially identical content sent to many recipients who did not ask to receive it is spam.

An authority on Usenet, W D Baseley, noted in 1998 that unsolicited bulk e-mail (UBE) was by then already the single largest form of e-mail abuse. He posted an 'FAQ' (frequently asked question) with the following information:

There are automated e-mail sending programs that can send millions of messages a day; the bandwidth, storage space, and time consumed by such massive mailing is incredible. One month's worth of mailings from one of the most nefarious bulk e-mail outfits was estimated at over 134 gigabytes, yes that's right, gigabytes. Each message was sent over the e-mail wires, consuming bandwidth. Then, each message was either stored locally or 'bounced' back to the sender, taking up storage space and even more bandwidth. Finally, each boxholder was forced to spend time dealing with the message.

These are all legitimate, measurable costs, and they are not borne by the sender of the messages. UBE is, at best, exploitation of e-mail for profit; at worst, theft. There are currently few regulations regarding UBE; the potential for growth is open-ended. All by itself, UBE could render the e-mail system virtually useless for legitimate messages.

Some would argue that there is such a thing as 'responsible' UBE; those who honour 'remove' requests and use the lists on 'Remove Me' or 'No Spam' Web sites would fit their description of 'responsible'. However, due to the types of messages contained in most UBE, and the historic lack of responsibility on the part of the sending organizations, UBE and Unsolicited Commercial E-mail (UCE) have earned a reputation as tawdry, widely unpopular methods of disseminating information.

Unsolicited commercial e-mail

This is widely used, and confused with UBE. UCE must be commercial in nature but does not imply massive numbers. Several ISPs specify a threshold for unsolicited commercial e-mail: sending one UCE is a violation.

In a specific case, individuals took offence at having been sent commercial messages regarding their Web sites. Their addresses were posted for the purpose of comments and suggestions about the site; the messages received were commercial offerings to buy ad space on the site or sell something to the site maintainer.

Falling into the spam trap is quite common. There are a lot of comments in Newsgroups fingering specific companies. The interesting thing is that this direct criticism is often not monitored by the culprit (marketing director) and the level of damage goes unnoticed.

SECURITY

The primary e-mail security issue is that someone can intercept and read your e-mail. E-mail is inherently insecure and can easily be read by people working for your organization's or Internet service provider's computer services department, and by the computer services department at the e-mail's destination. E-mail can also be read by any one of many people who have access to the many routers (Internet communications are controlled by routers which switch data from one network to another) along the path your e-mail takes to get to its destination.

It is possible that the source computer, destination computer, or any intervening router may have a program configured to automatically copy every e-mail that contains certain keywords for later review. For example, your organization may filter and trap e-mail that contains certain proprietary keywords, to check that nobody is revealing confidential information. Your addressee's company may have similar filters in place on their network.

It is not unusual for companies to monitor e-mail, and organizations have to inform employees that they are doing so. There have been many cases of people being fired for sending e-mail with adult content, such as adult jokes, when the company specifically had a policy in place against it.

Everyone in your organization should be made aware that e-mail is not secure without encryption. Your organization should be aware that even encryption has its limitations. E-mail to many countries is open to government scrutiny, and for inspection by secret services, religious sects, political parties and even local policemen.

SPOCS FROM HMG

In the UK, because of messy legislation (the Regulation of Investigatory Powers Act 2000) you and the organization's employees may be required (for the rest of their life) to reveal any passwords or the means for de-encryption they may use or have used to a multitude of quasi-autonomous government and non-government organizations on the say-so of the local police chief, or face imprisonment.

Roger Gaspar, deputy director-general of the National Criminal Intelligence Service, is trying to get public authorities and people who may be responsible for access to your organization's (and employees') private information to work through experts called 'Spocs' (a single point of contact in each of the authorized authorities like the local police or the Inland Revenue).

Your organization may locate hosting and a substantial part of competitively sensitive Internet interactive services in a country where competitive advantage is less threatened and will take precautions to ensure at least reasonable security, for sender and receiver. In the UK it is a moot point as to whether this is already prudent under the 'first duty of care' provisions in employment law.

Paranoid governments aside, e-mail security is largely a matter of corporate culture. Reasonable caution and peer group awareness and vigilance are the most potent means for making e-mail safe and secure. People, not technology, provide the best form of Internet security.

PERSONAL E-MAIL ISSUES

There are some personal e-mail hygiene rules that should be followed:

- frequently change your password;
- have different e-mails for different activities (it makes sense to have different intranet e-mail addresses);
- use numbers and both upper/lowercase letters in your passwords. It's easy to guess a password like 'MaryD', but it's much harder guessing a password like 'd45A15';
- don't leave a running machine unattended. Shut off or reboot any computer you've finished using. If you leave your computer unattended frequently throughout the day, download a screen saver with password protection for greater security.

Because unsolicited e-mail wastes so much time it is worth knowing about some of the products available to protect systems.

14

Newsgroups

The best recommendation I can make to practitioners who want to use or become active in newsgroups is to search 'newsgroups' at www.Yahoo.com. It offers a huge resource. This chapter puts much of that content into a PR context.

Usenet newsgroups, the discussion groups in which you can share information and opinions with people all over the world, are accessed with newsreaders or you can use a desktop newsreader such as Netscape Navigator or Internet Explorer.

NEWSGROUP TOOLS

Netscape Communicator 4.5 and above. To find and subscribe to newsgroups (in Netscape Communicator 4.5 and above), follow the steps below.

From the Communicator menu, select newsgroups. This will open a window for mail and news. Right-click the news server name in the navigation bar on the left. This will open a window listing all available newsgroups. Now you can search for your specific interests.

Internet Explorer 5.X To find and subscribe to newsgroups (in Internet Explorer), follow the steps below.

> From the Tools menu, select Mail and News, then Read News. This will open Outlook Express. Click the news server name on the left. Then, on the screen to the right, click the newsgroups button. This will bring up a window listing all available newsgroups.
>
> You can search for specific newsgroups by entering keywords in the 'Search for newsgroups that contain:' field, or browse the entire list. To subscribe to a newsgroup, highlight the group and click Subscribe.
>
> You can also visit a high number of newsgroups via Web interfaces such as Dejanews (http://www.deja.com/usenet).

There are a lot of groups, each with a special interest or focus. Some of them are very active, others less so. Some have not been used in years but the information is still available for anyone to access. Newsgroup information may have currency irrespective of its age.

Within each newsgroup, you'll find any number of articles on a given subject, and many subjects being discussed. Usenet newsgroups allow you to reply to articles you have read and to publish ('post'), in a few sentences, your own articles for others to read.

NEWS GROUP ETIQUETTE

Internet etiquette (netiquette) is written by J Chandler, the owner of 'Dark Mountain' (http://www.darkmountain.com). See also Emily (http://psg.com/emily.html); it is a masterpiece of irony with a lesson in every line. One further and authoritative source is at: http://www.albion.com/netiquette/.

Newsgroups differ widely in subject and style. Topics vary from Abba to zoology; content ranges from scientific discourse to casual letters between a small group of friends. With thousands of newsgroups available, there is something for everyone.

Newsgroups are organized into subject hierarchies, with the first few letters of the newsgroup name indicating the major subject category and sub-categories represented by a sub-topic name. Many subjects have multiple levels of sub-topics. Some major subject categories are: news, rec (recreation), soc (society), sci (science), comp (computers), and so forth; there are many more. Users can post to existing newsgroups, respond to previous posts (contributions to a newsgroup), and create new newsgroups.

Newcomers to newsgroups are requested to learn basic Usenet etiquette called 'netiquette' and users are also asked to get familiar with a newsgroup before posting information to it. An FAQ posting to the newsgroup is usually provided for 'newbies'. Some newsgroups have a designated person who decides which postings to allow or to remove and 'moderates' the group. Most newsgroups are unmoderated.

Using newsgroups as the means for disseminating messages for your organization is not easy. Many newsgroups are very clubby and resent apparent strangers attempting to interfere with 'their conversation'. Such resentment can have harsh repercussions on reputation. Newsgroups, when properly used, offer considerable opportunities to engage relevant, interested and active opinion-forming constituents.

There are software programs that allow organizations to send standard information such as advertisements directly to newsgroups automatically. It has to be said that unless applied with great care, this is probably the fastest way to wreck your reputation online. This is because the communication is direct with your selected audience and it is exactly where they can answer back to others who also have a direct interest in your organization.

Newsgroups are listed (and accessed) via a range of information providers. If you decide to participate in a newsgroup, it's best to first read a representative selection of articles over several days or even weeks before posting. This is called 'lurking'. Each newsgroup may have its own set of accepted guidelines for what constitutes an appropriate posting, and becoming familiar with the group before posting will help you show good manners and avoid offending others.

CREATE YOUR OWN NEWSGROUP

You can create your own newsgroup by following the instructions at: http://www.visi.com/~barr/alt-creation-guide.html or http://www.faqs.org/faqs/usenet/creating-newsgroups/part1/.

If you are new to Usenet, you should read the newsgroups' news.newusers.questions and news.announce.newusers to learn about technique and 'netiquette' before posting. To access this discussion list from a browser, go to www.dejanews.com/usenet, click on 'news' click into the 'new. newusers' link and then click on 'news.newusers.questions'.

You can also find a large repository of Usenet FAQ files for a wide variety of newsgroups online. It's best to read any existing FAQ for a newsgroup before posting so that you'll avoid irritating other readers by asking questions that have already been answered many times.

There are occasions when, to create a public forum, you may need to start your own newsgroup. In many instances, this is a very valuable and effective means for communication. It does make sense to have a good Internet presence before you begin to get involved. A Web site with good facts is very helpful as you exchange information with live but virtual neighbours.

Lots of PR people have been put off using newsgroups for communication. This is a shame. It's great fun and can be very valuable. Indeed lots of sites have their own discussion lists and they can be very lively places too.

REACHING INTO NEWSGROUPS

One of the quickest ways for a company to become evident in newsgroups is to make a mistake.

Powergen's disclosure of its customers' credit card details on its Web site generated hundreds of comments in newsgroups. One contributor had only ever posted two comments to a newsgroup. One of the correspondents responding to this posting had a record of making 1,680 postings to 46 different newsgroups; another one had a history of 600 postings to 32 different groups. We see the network of networks in action and capable of carrying messages round the Internet about a single issue affecting one company. For every person who contributes to a newsgroup there may be scores (even hundreds) who just view the content. The audience profile is of aware, educated, articulate and relatively wealthy people.

Historically, such comments may have been made in a social context such as a bar. It may have been through the moderated content of a letter to a newspaper. On the Internet comment has a massive audience potential and is probably not moderated. The only hope for an organization is that there are so many postings that most people will not see all of the content. However, people using the Internet seek information and 'pull' it.

Newsgroups are powerful both for good and ill. Managing presence in newsgroups is important for reputation managers. Being proactive is possible, even desirable, but needs to be undertaken in the full knowledge of the potential consequences. There will be tension between the marketer and the reputation manager over the use of newsgroups for promotional purposes and the PR approach needs closer scrutiny. But when you or your organization even contemplate such activities (and this is as much a guide for marketers as PR professionals), work on the assumption that you will lose some customers, prospects and goodwill in the process. Advertising in some newsgroups is like putting billboards up at a football match but in others it is like driving a Ferrari into the British Library.

The methods used to identify newsgroups and even e-mail addresses to allow you to provide information should include a request in the newsgroup/s asking users if they would like to be included in the distribution of relevant news, issues, products, white papers, etc.

Remember that in newsgroups, as for e-mail (but in the knowledge that newsgroup participants can easily bite back), no means *no*. Newsgroups are not a place for advertisements, including job vacancies and self-promotion. It is acceptable to respond to a request but users seldom appreciate pushed information. Pushy promotion happens and then either the members become angry or they actively set out to block spammers or go and form a new group where promotion is not allowed.

The specific nature of newsgroups is such that interference in their exchanges can be resented. The best analogy is that of a stranger joining a conversation among friends in a bar. There are considerable advice resources available online, as mentioned above.

There are some groups out there that allow advertising in the posts. Some groups welcome representatives of companies and other organizations, but many/most don't. Newsgroup users begin to formulate opinions of other members based on their questions and responses. They participate in groups that relate to their specific interests. They tell people where they work and what they do. But if all you are contributing is corporate speak or a product

---

Re: Test Equipment Calibration Services   more options

Author: Harry H Conover
Email: conover@tiac.net
Date: 1998/09/11
Forums: alt.industrial,computing, sci,electronics.design, sci.elec-
               tronics.misc, Sci.engr.mech

more headers

Jeff (jeffq@ptp.hp.com) wrote:
:acctmgr@my-dejanews.com wrote:
:>Be sure to visit our Web site at: http://www.simco.com
:>>Simply stated, SIMCO provides the highest value in quality
  calibration and
:>>data management service available today!
:>>
:>>SIMCO is the largest commercial provider of metrology services
  in the United
:>>States, with laboratories coast to coast. Wherever you are and
  whatever your
:
:Did we really need this SPAM??

No, but if they give Green Trading Stamps for reading their SPAM, I'm
willing to put up with it. ;-)

They don't? In that case I believe we should Black-list the SPAMMING
B*****DS across the entire scientific and industrial community!

Still, is it possible that the SIMCO outfit accidentally hired some
wet-behind-the-ears kid, or coop student who, without their knowledge, is out to make a name for himself but...as it turns out...at
their expense?

Figure 14.1

puff, it's not going to work. If you are a knowledgeable person whom people come to trust or respect, they will talk to you if they think they need your services or can enjoy sharing your knowledge.

Research topics of interest to the group so that the advice and information you provide is relevant and educated. This means that to be effective, you must go beyond simple discursive contribution and build a strong reputation by providing relevant, useful and high-quality information that the group can use.

In newsgroups, as in other forms of communication and advertising, you have to obey the basic rule of knowing your customers and understanding what they need.

SOME DOS AND DON'TS

Everyone is tempted to blurt out their belief of the truth, or to challenge the views of another contributor head on, or even to tell the whole group that they are wrong. Few have managed to do this without creating a storm of protest and sometimes very angry responses that have echoed round Usenet. Flaming (violent expressions of disapproval), misunderstandings, overreactions, and hurt feelings are par for the course. There are four lessons from experience:

1. Be polite. When in Rome, do as the Romans. Offer an opinion courteously.
2. If there is misunderstanding, apologize. As in real life people who are quick to anger are often equally quick to forgive.
3. Don't be drawn. It is relatively easy to get someone to respond in haste and write a post that will upset and anger the group. Lurk a while before you respond and establish the mood of the group.
4. Defer to the establishment. In every Usenet newsgroup and listserv mailing list there are people who have earned the respect of everyone in the group. Many of them will be expert, well informed and will have considerable experience.

There are some things to remember such as indicating what you're responding to. Quote (briefly) or paraphrase. If the original 'Subject:' line was 'Big dogs' make sure yours says 'Re: Big dogs'. Some reply functions do this automatically. By Net convention, included lines are preceded by '>' (greater than signs). Some mail editors and newsreaders do this automatically. Here are some more tips:

● Use normal capitalization. Separate your paragraphs with blank lines.
● Don't betray confidences. It is all too easy to quote a personal letter or e-mail in a posting to the entire group. If you want to be associated with a comment, give reasons. Simply saying 'I agree' can be out of context.
● Don't make statements about your organization that it may have to react to unless you are sure of your ground (my company X is discounting Rolls Royce cars). Someone may take you up on it.
● Don't SEND A MESSAGE IN ALL CAPS. Capital letters are considered to be the equivalent of shouting and are difficult to read.

- Using comedy, satire, sarcasm and idioms as well as analogies can be hazardous. Newsgroups are global and most such posts do not translate well. In addition it is very easy to be misunderstood.
- It is always a risk to start a new topic (called a 'thread'). The group may have just finished a long, bitter war about that very subject. But if you want to take the risk, say something yourself about the subject you're raising.
- Never pretend you're anything other than who you are. Group members want to help you to answer a question, help you find information.

THE LANGUAGE OF NEWSGROUPS

Threads are a string of responses to a single message. Rather than starting a new message, continue threads by using the 'Reply' function in your e-mail programme. By maintaining threads, it's easier to follow the flow of information, especially after dozens of messages are exchanged.

There are a lot of newsgroup posts that are an amazingly long single, and unreadable, line. Rather than capital letters, try use asterisks to add *emphasis* whenever possible. When sending a URL in the body of a message use the full Internet convention, eg: http://www.netreputation.net. And turn off the HTML settings! Many e-mail programs send your e-mail in the form of a Web page so you can embed links, sounds, graphics, etc.

The rules for discussion lists seem severe. They are. The reason is that they are where reputations are made and marred without the PR practitioner adding fuel to the fire. Well-conducted PR inside newsgroups can be exceptionally rewarding and the returns can be very high, but they do need dedicated and committed handling by responsible people who want to help newsgroup members and who can meet Internet constituents halfway. This is not to say that the organization should be compromised or should compromise its standards, but that its nature and aims will be clearly understood and respected.

With such warnings and rules in mind, newsgroups offer many opportunities. It is always best to use an expert rather than a proxy to join debates and it is important that if you post a comment, you must watch for any response. And, of course, it's great fun.

15

Constituent relationship management

CUSTOMER RELATIONSHIP MANAGEMENT

Throughout this book there are examples of how one may build relationships with publics. Relationships with customers are very important and there is significant investment in technology and applications to make it effective online.

The concepts and processes of customer relationship management (CRM) are important to PR practice. It is an area of relationship management and, thereby part of the PR portfolio. In addition, the principles of re-engineering corporate processes and bending the organization to respond to the will of customers, creating new one-to-one relationships and the associated and valuable technologies are all ready made for the application of PR.

PR is about much more than customer relations and while CRM is naturally focused on customers, the PR practitioner has to view such relationships for a much wider constituency. We talk of customer relationship management but, in doing so, you may like to project the idea into constituency relationships management. After all, why should customer have all the fun?

People become deeply engaged in what they are doing in cyberspace. Its ability to respond to commands and open a feast of information is part of its interest. In addition, the technology interacts in a quasi-personal way. Furthermore, actions by its users can provoke interaction with large organizations, groups and individuals. Anyone can make a company send him or her an e-mail – *wow!*

It did not take the commercial users of the Internet long to discover that there was also an opportunity for organizations to tailor responses to user interests and needs. This form of interaction was in place when the majority of Internet users where academics. Commercial interest and the financial muscle that went with the enthusiasm for the Net pushed out the envelope of this idea into marketing. Interactive selling to a niche consumer market became what is now known as customer relationship marketing.

HOW CRM WORKS

As users interact within Web sites, information is collected and collated in databases. Computer programs create user models, a sort of character set about the person who has visited the Web site plus information coming in from cookies and marketing data. These programs then create packages of information, dressed up with offerings and presentations that are relevant to the user. This, largely with the connivance and consent of the user, allows interaction to be proactive on both sides. E-mail marketing and pre-configured Web offerings begin to emerge to the satisfaction of both parties.

Example such as My Yahoo!, Microsoft's 'My Communities', My Deja and Amazon's 'My account' all greet the user by name. Their details, specific activities and interests become immediately available. These properties also provide tailored services such as free Web sites and hosting, news and opportunities to do things such as (surprise, surprise) buy products and services. When entering such personalized properties, an enhanced relationship is created. Such relationships ensure return visits and further opportunities to sell.

There is a lot of software available to help. Of course, what these programs cannot do is provide a true one-to-one relationship. They are the functional processes on the way to creating an understanding, accommodation or empathy between an organization and, ideally, all its constituents.

Many software packages offer advanced and sophisticated processes to narrow the gap between broadcast and narrowcast communication. Progressively they get smarter to make the approach to individuals a closer match to their apparent needs. There are pitfalls on the way. The first list and marketing of such services can be very broad and inaccurate and closer to spam than relationship management. Of more significance, they are not capable of being flexible enough to appreciate the many and complex motivations of individuals. Even people find that hard. The computer programs have the advantage of a better and longer memory and tireless attention to duty when real people are asleep, but they are quite inept at understanding semiotics. That is not to say that PR practitioners should not attempt to harness these capabilities well beyond the boundaries of relationship marketing. They should.

The application of these techniques to enrich experience between an organization and its constituents over a wide range of issues is important. Its importance is reinforced every time an organization applies CRM because of the need to satisfy the many and wide-ranging societal, political and personal contexts which are also in play when people start to build an interactive relationship with the organization's Web site or Internet property.

Many organizations promise CRM solutions. Many even propose to put such solutions in place in a very short time or to a deadline. This is not possible. Most of the technology may be in place quickly. In addition the process of relationship building can cover a lot of ground in months, but then and thereafter there is a refinement process that is never-ending. Some people do fit in neat and proscribed profiles, most don't. They need to be considered as more than a socio-economic class or a geo-lifestyle consumer because when they do not seem to fit, on the Internet, they go elsewhere.

While CRM is about rationalizing your customer base, for example getting rid of customers who are costing you money and keeping customers who will add to the bottom line, PR constituency management (PRCM) has to view constituents in a wider context (see issues-driven constituents in Chapter 10).

CRM SOFTWARE

There are software packages to aid the process. The better recognized ones include Siebel (http://www.siebel.com) and Peoplesoft (http://www.peoplesoft.com) for a sales force automation system; Remedy for a helpdesk system; Davox (http://www.davox.com) for a call centre system; eGain (http://www.egain.com) to sort e-mails coming in over the Web; and BroadVision (http://www.broadvision.com) for visible offerings to the user. The practitioner should not stop at these providers: there are many other companies with excellent products.

The key to implementing PRCM may well start with a CRM; preferably, it will start long before then. CRM requires a lot of thought long before technology is considered and PRCM has to be driven from a concept of relationship building between the organization and its many constituents. Inevitably it will be part of a wider PR strategy and will be multi-channel in nature. There are considerable offline considerations. Joined-up relationship and reputation management is critical for all organizations. If the two are not in sync, there will be tears.

As with CRM, practitioners will need to look at what business processes have to be changed, re-engineered and optimized before they start looking at any technology. The technology is there only to fulfil business requirements and will probably require the services of a systems integrator (just as CRM does).

The business consultancy Strategy Partners says that CRM is a 'business ethic, not a technology issue' and KPMG, and others, talk of the 'CRM ethos' and the concept of a market of one. By this they mean that the marketing process is aimed at becoming a one-to-one relationship. For most (all) organizations, this is not possible but it is an excellent goal. Without taking the first steps in this direction no achievement will be made and competitors will have an inbuilt opportunity and advantage.

It is absolutely impossible for every single person who comes to your organization's Web site to be treated as an individual, and yet

Dell, the computer retailer, has a very good CRM model that is individual and specific to its Web site visitors and online customer needs. It presents its offering in such a way that you feel as if you are getting exactly what you want. Similarly, everybody thinks that when they use My Yahoo! they are getting their own personalized front page. This is an illusion, but very effective.

By applying the CRM model to the wider practice of PR, the experience for the visitor can be richer and can add significantly to CRM while aiming at the target of enhanced understanding and a deeper relationship with constituents. PRCM has the power to create highly integrated relationships of an order of magnitude better for an organizations because it affects so many stakeholders if not achieving the goal of one-to-one relationships with all stakeholders. To have a similar commitment to an organization from vendors, local communities, employees and customers all focused on its success, is a PR goal worth going for.

B2B RELATIONSHIP MARKETING

It will come as no surprise to PR practitioners that the marts, exchanges, auctions and catalogues that make up the majority of the business-to-business (B2B) e-commerce infrastructure lack content.

A large number of practitioners work in the B2B sector and so this area of Internet development is important to them. It is supposed to create markets where commercial buyers and sellers can find each other, and purchase goods and services. In principle, there are big advantages. The cost of marketing and selling (especially employment of a sales force, and distribution chain relationships) are saved and the reach of the Internet offers new and global markets. Equally, buyers save on the high cost of running a purchasing department and can compare cost, specification, quality and delivery and buy from a global vendor base.

In practice suppliers say that they are finding it prohibitively difficult to sell on these sites because of the number of different marketplaces and the different catalogue formats required by each marketplace. The provision and management of content is seen as key to the success of online marketplaces but the lack of standardization is causing suppliers to be disillusioned. The ability to offer products in marts and catalogues in the form they require has to be taken seriously. These processes need to be standardized to work and provide benefits to both sides. In addition, because there are so many outlets, the information demanded has to be reformatted many times over. This is largely an issue of database management.

B2B marketing does not stop there. There is also a requirement to offer products on Web sites and other Internet properties for prospective customers to view and buy. The ability to buy effectively requires forms of data collection, collation and management and effective relationship building with prospective suppliers.

There is a third ingredient. The relationship and reputation management of these processes through understanding of the relevant constituents, the processes for creating relationships, consequential enhancements in development of Web site and other forms of content for both purchasers and marketing are PR issues. It is no longer good enough for PR departments to say that 'Purchasing is in charge of vendor relations.' One might ask, 'Why not put the purchasing function in charge of press relations?' Supplier relationship management is a PR activity and never more so than on the Internet.

Your organization will build relationships with such enterprises. Some will be very visible because they interface with the public; examples are recruitment sites and advertising space buying portals, while others will be less obvious because they specialize, for example, paper or metal exchanges. Practitioners will discover that their organization is progressively using more of these exchanges in building relationships for everything from stationery to steel. You will find the number and range of affected Internet constituents are both large in number and highly effective in influencing opinion.

The significance of these exchanges is that the users are a tight-knit group and highly interconnected. Furthermore, their opinions and views when expressed in the bulletin boards and chats embedded within the sites are highly focused on narrow publics with immense and direct influence over your organization. There is an added dimension, which is that such comments can quickly be transferred into the wider Internet and can have a dramatic influence on the wider constituency.

While the relationships may, on the surface, be different, the rules of good Internet PR, outlined in this book, still apply.

16

The reach of Internet news

News is very important for the Internet. Nearly every user of the Internet receives news via it.

In the United States, reading online news is reported to be Internet users' second favourite online activity after e-mail (according to a survey from the Zatso, Inc and the Radio and Television News Directors Foundation in July 2000). A survey by Juniper Communications (http://www.jup.com) shows that more than 80 per cent of US online consumers trust online news as much as the more traditional news outlets, such as newspapers, television and cable news. An additional 7 per cent view online news as more reliable than other media.

In the UK, where reading newspapers is by tradition more pervasive, most people do not use or want to use the Internet as their first choice source for news, according to a survey by the business information Web site Just-sites.com (http://www.just-sites.com). It reports that only 20 per cent of Internet users prefer to catch up on news using the Web (about 3.6 million people). However, when it comes to the world of work and business, the survey discovered, people are fed up with the number of print titles they are expected to read – there are over 6,000 business titles in the UK – and are turning to the Internet to cope. One in five business respondents agrees that the Internet is a better way to receive news than conventional trade press, primarily because it is faster. One suspects that, as the cost of Internet access in the UK and Europe falls, there may be a trend towards the US model.

Because there is a lot of news available across the Internet very few people are willing to pay for it. In the UK less than 3 per cent of Internet users are prepared to pay. This may be because news is one of the most popular added features for Web sites. News can be added to Web sites from a range of online news vendors easily and inexpensively (much content is free). The reason for including news in a site is that news vendors allow the Webmaster to configure a bespoke news feed that is relevant to the Web site visitors, which encourages revisits and makes a site look up to date and current.

HOW INTERNET NEWS IS READ

Online news reading patterns differ greatly from those for newspapers and magazines, according to a study from the Poynter Institute and Stanford University. People reading news on Internet sites tend to focus on the article text first, looking at photos and graphics afterwards. Those who read newspapers and magazines do the opposite: look at illustrations first then read the text.

THE POYNTER INSTITUTE STUDY OF NEWS READERSHIP ONLINE

Will Internet news readers give up serendipity? If they narrow their sources, will they stop encountering stories they hadn't intended to read? Will this cut down on their knowledge of the world? See http://www.poynter.org/eyetrack2000/index.htm.

The first Poynter Institute research programme showed that the subjects read both mainstream general news sources and traditional speciality news providers. They had often tried customized news, but had given that up 'because I might miss something I ought to know about'. They read multiple news sites in about 30-minute sessions. They became news junkies and were also still reading newspapers and magazines and listening to radio news. Most of them had been reading online news for about a year or less.

The second research project, two years later, used eye-tracking equipment that recorded where the eyes stopped to absorb information identified subjects read. The project found that fewer of the people studied appear to be news junkies in the second two-year project compared to the first. Subjects often did not subscribe to daily papers or do much TV news viewing but continued to listen to radio news programmes; they had cancelled some magazine subscriptions. Most had been reading online for two or more years and did not like customized news much, for the same reason as before: they might miss 'something important'.

Is there no end to the demand for content? The news reader on the Internet is always looking for more just as all users seem to. Is it a surprise that Internet users are worse that TV channel hoppers when there is so much not to be missed? This may suggest there is an insatiable demand for news.

THE NEWS GENERATORS

There are three sorts of Internet news:

1. The news that comes from established sources such as Reuters (http://www.reuters.com), offline publications with an online presence like the *Financial Times* (FT.com (http://www.ft.com), the BBC (http://www.bbc.co.uk) and online media such as Motley Fool (http://www.fool.com) and Silicon.com (http://www.silicon.com), which do not have a printed version.
2. News from sources that have less provenance and can be merely the stories and opinions of individuals made available to the public via a Web site.
3. Organizations as a source of news. They provide their own online media stories, which can also be followed and re-distributed round the Net.

These sources for news can be presented either as an 'exclusive' resource without a ready means for its redistribution or they can be offered as a news feed to Webmasters using simple technologies to allow them to be reused on a third party site or on a number of news sites and portals.

The interesting thing about Internet news distribution is that an organization may be creating its own news and, at the same time, may be redistributing news from other (sometimes several) sources. The many good examples of this process in action have one thing in common. The news is up to the minute.

MEDIA LIST PROVIDERS

The online and offline media are rapidly becoming one and the same thing. Here are some sources:

http://www.romeike.com
http://www.prnet.co.uk
http://www.mediainfo.co.uk/prnewslink/prnewslink.htm
http://www.ukbusinessnet.com/datafile/x-media.htm
http://www.pa.press.net/
http://www.pressreleasenetwork.com/page.htm

However, it has to be remembered that the quality and modernity of news distributed via Web sites (and other Internet delivery platforms and channels) is up to the Web site owner. There are some that offer unreliable or out of date news and some that add comments that may be suspect.

Standards for Internet news distribution

The global news reporting industry has moved so deeply into electronic media and digital formats that the Geneva-based International Press Telecommunications Council (IPTC) has been developing a scheme to aid news distribution. It's called NewsML.

The new digital language structures multimedia news so it can be delivered to devices ranging from PCs to mobile phones. IPTC has already launched NewsML (http://www.newsml.org) which is a relatively new but already popular XML-based standard to represent and manage news throughout its lifecycle, including production, interchange and consumer use

---

NEWSML HIGHLIGHTS

The IPTC (http://www.iptc.org) has adopted the NewsML standard for formatting electronic content. NewsML is based on eXtensible Markup Language, XML. NewsML is an XML encoding for news, which is intended to be used for the creation, transfer, delivery and archiving of news.

NewsML is media independent, and allows equally for the representation of the evening TV news and a simple textual story.

With journalism becoming increasingly digital, and with a proliferation of database archives, NewsML is designed to assist news organizations in putting together multimedia stories, adapting them, storing them and retrieving them later. The PR industry will need to use such international standards to assist news outlets and reporters.

The news vendors

Placing news on Web sites needs considerable research.

The importance of knowing where the news is actually generated is critical. Sending a press release to, for example, Yahoo! is not very productive: it does not take all the output from all its news sources. It (electronically) selects the news it will offer on its site. Yahoo! is one of the most powerful news distributors in the world but it is not a generator of any news (except as a company in its own right).

There are a lot of virtual news vendors. The number could be in the order of hundreds of thousands. Some add comment and facts to breaking news, so a story originating from Reuters or PR Newswire (http://www.prnewswire.com) can be relayed and commented on and may be supplemented with related news and comment from other third parties.

The news brokers

There are an almost uncountable number of news sources available from the Internet and there are organizations that collect, collate and index news and then repackage it for use by news outlets, Web site owners and other news distributors (online and offline).

They offer services that sometimes include original editorial as well as redistributed news that can be configured by Webmasters to be relevant to specific site visitors and pipe it directly on to these sites. It is often very difficult to identify the original source for such news.

In some cases, the range of news feeds these news brokers include is so big, that identifying their sources and the selection criteria used is unfathomable.

NEWS BROKERS

The following links may be informative:
www.screamingmedia.com, www.lsyndicate.com and
www.moreover.com.

Two other news brokers are http://www.newshub.com and http://www.yellowbrix.com/index.html. A personalized new broker is Crayon http://crayon.net/.

There are also specialist brokers including http://www.business-wire.com/ Newsbytes.com, Newshub, providing news to corporate Web sites such as DayTraders.com, LookAheadCharts.com, The Stock Advisor.com, Global Stock Advisor.com, MetaMoney.com, SearchCarribean, Cyber Week Comm, Inc., Avid Trading, Beacon Trading, DayTrading.com, Internet Stock News, A B Watley, Insider Street, AboveTrade.com and TD Waterhouse Institutional. It is a big business.

In addition there are a number of specific news search engines like News junkies, News Index and NewsNow.

Added content resource

The practice of adding information to news stories is another form of news distribution. News generators such as CNN and the BBC practise this. Sometimes this is overt and sometimes it requires close inspection to identify these additional news sources.

Taking the BBC as an example, many stories will provide a list of other Internet sources that may add to the content provided by

BBC news. At the time when Concorde crashed in France on 25 July, 2000, killing 113 people, the BBC story (http://news.bbc. co.uk/hi/english/world/europe/newsid_855000/855191.stm) provided a link to 'the Unofficial Concorde Home Page', which is run by David Trebosc (http://www.geocities. com/CapeCanaveral/Lab/8952/e_index.htm).

This is an exciting opportunity for practitioners because they are best placed to offer news outlets with all this added richness. There is competitive advantage to be gained from the potential to endorse organization, event, brand, product or service as well as provide an excellent service to journalists and editors. A cursory look at most online news outlets will demonstrate the extent to which this practice of adding enhanced richness with referral sites is now common if not de rigueur.

The news distributors

Many news vendors, brokers and organizations also offer an additional means for delivering news. E-mail distribution of breaking news is very common and allows users to invite a news supplier to send e-mail notification of breaking news, daily news and news summaries direct to their in-box, WAP phone, kiosk, ticker, etc.

This service can be made to be very specific, a bespoke service to the individual concerned. Many portals offer these services, including the big search engines such as Yahoo! and Excite.

It will not come as a great surprise to know that some of these news items are redistributed by the individual concerned throughout corporate intranets and to a wider, even global, network of friends and colleagues.

For PR practitioners, understanding the process of news distribution is very important. Knowing where news originated and how it flows round the Internet is important if they wish to influence the online media agenda.

The new news

The newly extended global nature of news, the proliferation of sources of news, not to mention the sources to access news is a revolution that has occurred in the space of a few months.

In the meantime, the media has to be much more transparent. The Internet audience is well aware and often ahead of the media with the news. Trust is important for news outlets, which can be subject to heavyweight criticism when their activities are not up to the mark.

Commercial Alert
1611 Connecticut Ave, NW Suite #3A
Washington, DC 20009
202 296 2787 Phone 202 833 2406 Fax
www.essential.org/alert alert@essential.org

May 31, 2000

Paul Steiger
Managing Editor
The Wall Street Journal
200 Liberty Street
New York, NY 10281-1003
via telecopier (212) 416-2658

Dear Mr. Steiger

We want to inquire about your newspaper's policies regarding secret agreements to exclude certain points of view from articles in exchange for a news scoop about corporations.

On May 29, The Washington Post reported a most troubling example of this trend. It said a publicist hired by United Airlines and US Airways offered three major newspapers a deal that none of them could refuse. The pitch: 'We'll give you the exclusive details of a $5 billion merger if you promise not to call any outsiders for comment.' According to the Post article, The Wall Street Journal, New York Times and Washington Post all agreed, but the deal fell apart because the Financial Times broke the story on its Web site.

These secret exclusion agreements with corporations or their PR firms limit the scope of discussion of a news story about corporate conduct. They block out voices that offer perspective on corporations, such as consumer, citizen, public health, or environmental groups. For example, the deal with airline's PR firm excluded comment from anyone who might have questioned whether the airline merger was good citizens, consumers or the nation's free enterprise ideas.

Even worse, these secret agreements betray readers' trust. By failing to disclose the nature and extent of these agreements, readers do not know what information newspapers - which are supposed to provide news and analysis - are purposely hiding from them.

By adopting such secret agreements, your newspaper basically tells the story the corporate subject wants you to tell while pretending to be an objective news source. Other voices are excluded entirely from the discussion and debate, even though the corporate conduct in question may affect them personally and deeply. This in turn sends an implicit message that these other voices aren't worth hearing, and so they may not get heard at all.

Your readers deserve to know the answers to these question:
1. What is your policy regarding the disclosure of agreements to exclude perspectives, in exchange for a news scoop about a corporation?
2. Would your newspaper agree to running a box under a news story disclosing any secret exclusion agreements, indication what points of view have been intentionally omitted?

Sincerely,

George Gerbner, President and Founder, Cultural Environment Movement, Dean Emeritus, Annenberg School of Communication
Janine Jackson, Program director, Fairness and Accuracy in Reporting (FAIR)
Robert McChesney, Research Associate Professor, U of Illinois at Urbana-Champaign, author, Rich Media, Poor Democracy
Mark Crispin Miller, Professor of Media Ecology, New York University
Gary Ruskin, Directror, Commercial Alert
John Stauber, Executive Director, Center for Media Democracy

Figure 16.1 *The movement of news*

This has significant implications for the PR industry. The Internet invites news media to be more accurate and comprehensive, which means they have to be less accepting of spin.

The media outlets have proliferated and the uptake is global. Practitioner activities are open to scrutiny by worldwide audiences. Media competition is as much for veracity and thus valuable trust, as for reach. And the interest in any single outlet can now be very narrow but exceptionally expert. Targeting the subject matter as well as the means for distribution has new meaning for practitioners aiming to have an effect on their core constituents.

The news media are in competition with the news on your Web site. If the content of your site is accurate, transparent and truthful, and written in the language of your constituents, journalists cannot afford to be inaccurate. There is significant evidence to show that the accuracy of news and media reporting in general has been enhanced because of the Web site information now available to all.

COMMUNICATION WITH JOURNALISTS USING THE INTERNET

One of the most effective ways of promoting your online presence as well as enhancing overall image is via the online media. In addition, the traditional and much loved print media is now becoming wired. Its journalists use the Internet. Many publications provide even more extensive coverage online than in print versions and the news does not wait for the presses to roll: it is posted straight to the Web.

This means that for both online and offline media, the PR practitioner has to become proficient in online media relations.

The Internet is important to journalists

According to Global Financial Communication Network (http://www.gfcnet.com) almost 80 per cent of journalists have their work published over the Internet. This is more common in the UK, Germany and the United States, but shows how important the Internet has become for journalism.

JOURNALIST RESEARCH

Resources about journalism in general are:
http://www.ithaca.edu/library/htmls/journalism.html and
http://www.soi.city.ac.uk/~pw/ji_pubs.html.

UK research for the Internet conference for journalists
NetMedia2000; also this research:
http://www.thestandard.com/article/display/0,1151,20942,00.
html.

The US annual survey by Middleberg/Ross (The Middleberg/Ross
Print Media in Cyberspace Study)
http://www.middleberg.com;
http://www.middleberg.com/middlebergnews/view_pressrelease.
cfm?pressrelease_index=147.

A survey of French journalists shows uptake:
http://www.communicor.fr/English/Webstudy.html.

US technology journalist research can be found at:
http://www.politis.com/news/news7.htm.

Internet mediated journalism is explained at:
http://www.freepint.co.uk/issues/210199.htm?FreePint_Session
=a858ad9135c8f715f0ec3ca4793d75e4.

The views of a wired journalist are at:
http://www.davidlidsky.com/what_i_am_working_on.htm and
http://www.mediainfo.com/ephome/news/newshtm/stories/
051100n1.htm.

Where online editorial is heading is discussed at:
http://ajr.newslink.org/mmcol2.html and
http://www.onlinenewsassociation.org/links.html.

Around the world most journalists (86 per cent) are reported to
have access to e-mail but surprisingly a third said they hardly use
it at all and 40 per cent said one quarter of their communication
now takes place via e-mail.

US and UK journalists are comfortable with both e-mail and the Internet. They are more willing to make use of e-mail with their PR contacts. Their work is the most widely published on the Internet.

How journalists use the Net

Journalism is rapidly taking the Internet to heart. Some of the key findings help us understand what is significant to PR practitioners.

According to the Net Media 2000 research 62.7 per cent of journalists, excluding freelances, had Internet access from their personal computer. This means that most journalists have direct Internet access and those with an Internet connection on their desk were more likely to include online research material in their stories. Twenty-six per cent of journalists with access to personal computers used the Internet to research over 50 per cent of their stories.

Trade magazine journalists were more likely to use their connection to research material from 'e-mail news services' and 'e-mail press releases' compared to consumer magazines. For example, 35 per cent of trade stories were researched from 'e-mail news services' and 'E-mail press releases' were accessed the most to generate stories, followed by use of 'search engines' and 'Web news sites'. 'Newsgroups' were accessed the least to research story content. Freelances were more likely to use 'newsgroups' compared to staff journalists.

Among all the groups of journalists polled, e-mail was regarded as the most important function of the Internet, followed by 'information searches', while 'Finding sources' was the most important benefit of the Internet for 68 per cent of journalists, and 63 per cent put 'speed of information gathering' as the most important benefit.

In some media sectors, journalists reported that 25 per cent of the content of their stories was derived exclusively from the Internet. This is a very significant finding for the PR industry. Where a press relations agency or in-house office is not using the Internet, then the move by journalists towards using the Internet denies such organizations an equivalent amount of influence. Put another way, the press relations industry now using the Internet is denying its clientele of (even in 2000, 25 per cent for some media sectors) access to coverage.

If a journalist wants to know about your organization he or she will go the your Web site – first. When your organization is newsworthy, journalists will know your Web site intimately, even as intimately as you! This finding is significant for the PR practitioner for four reasons:

1. Is the practitioner making information available to journalists via the Internet and if not is the practitioner prepared to forego the opportunity to be included?
2. What exactly is available across the Internet about the organization, which journalists might find and use?
3. To what extent is the practitioner in a position to influence content that is (freely) available and that is not provided by the organization directly or indirectly?
4. To what extent is the practitioner making it easy for journalists to access information?

One can reasonably conclude that once journalists have access to the Internet (and most do), they will use it for a range of activities including getting ideas to research and for accessing information from organizations. Of course, whereas in the past they may have done this through the PR office, today they will expect the information from a Web site or other Internet source. Being able to find current information on Web sites is important for journalists.

JOURNALISTS' RESOURCES

Typical journalist resources: www.Prnet.co.uk; MediaNet; and ProfNet.

Depending on where the PR practitioner is working, the Internet is significant. For those with lots of news of interest to national newspapers, radio and television as well as online and trade and technical media, Internet relationships are a must. In the consumer and local media, the significance of the Internet had not become so critical at the time of the research.

This is reflected in the titles that are available online. The consumer titles in the UK were among the slowest to include any or any significant content online. Not surprisingly, a range of sites unrelated to the publishing industry, but aimed at comparable consumer markets, appeared to fill the gap. In turn such Internet sites may be relevant as targets for information from PR practitioners.

Plainly put, if a publication is not available online there will be another Internet property filling that gap in the market and that property should be your online target.

EMERGING TRENDS IN REPORTING

The United States has shown a consistent uptake of the Internet as a tool by journalists. By 2000 almost 75 percent of all US journalists used the Internet daily, up from 48 percent in the previous year. The June 2000 Middleberg/Ross survey showed that overall use of the Internet by US journalists was growing significantly, especially for article research, development of story ideas and sources, and for communicating with readers. E-mail had become more popular both for communicating with known sources as well as readers. New technologies also enjoyed a surge in popularity, with a quarter of respondents reporting use of instant messaging.

JOURNALISTS REPORT ONLINE RUMOUR

Don Middleberg, CEO of Middleberg + Associates reported that: 'Journalists are playing by new rules – developing story ideas online, reporting online rumours, and going to corporate and association Web sites for information especially when a story breaks.'

Credibility is emerging as a key issue. Some journalists are adding Internet rumours to add some spice to reporting and to how journalists found story ideas.

ACCREDITATION, PLAGIARISM AND STRAIGHT COPYING

There are some dangerous trends emerging too. 'While it is good that reporters' use of the Internet continues to expand, questionable ethical practices are also expanding,' according to Professor

---

Steven Ross of Columbia University School of Journalism who conducts the research with Don Middleberg. CEO of Middleberg and Associates.

'Media Web sites freely link to advertisers and to previously published articles, often failing to credit other publications' work,' he says. 'Many respondents also admitted to publishing rumours, often with little or no substantiation, and to using online sources whose credibility had not been adequately established.'

Silicon.com, an online e-zine, has faced this problem in the UK. One of its news stories was quoted by the *Sunday Times* with no attribution, a circumstance that would not pertain to an offline title. Once the error was pointed out the *Sunday Times* revised its approach. It seems there was an assumption that the Internet means we can leave the normal rules of civilization this side of the screen.

Journalists' use of the Internet is a major issue for the press relations sector of the PR industry. Some of the emerging findings in current research in the United States is significant for the UK.

Article research is the most popular use of the Internet, displacing e-mail and showing a clear use of the Net for adding depth and breadth to stories. Internet use for finding images is common for half the journalists responding. The use of the Internet for the development of story ideas is rising dramatically and journalists are reading publications online more frequently.

New technologies are becoming increasingly popular, with 25 per cent of respondents reporting use of instant messaging (AOL Instant Messenger, ICQ, Yahoo! Pager, etc), although only 6 per cent use it daily. Also, journalists are adopting on-screen news tickers, which provide news headlines even when a Web browser is turned off. Journalists find that responding to readers via e-mail is part of the job.

The conclusion one comes to is that the Internet is very important to journalists and is influencing how they develop and research stories. The findings in the United States suggest that the extension of use by journalists requires close attention to rumour as well as one's own content and the content provided by online partners, competitors and third parties.

APPROACHING WIRED JOURNALISTS

Of course, knowing the publication, whether it is on- or offline or both, is a basic requirement for all media relations practitioners. This includes reading it! Many practitioners are still taken by surprise to find the extent to which there is online, unique and comprehensive coverage associated with established offline titles and, in addition, that there is an extensive media which, though online, has no print counterpart.

Some established titles have a very different online presence and they can be confusing for the ill informed. The long-established *Yachting Monthly*, one would be forgiven for believing, is a monthly special interest magazines. Wrong! It is a daily publication online and a monthly journal as the printed version.

Relations with journalists are now changing and there is a greater emphasis on good media relationship management. It is significant to make sure that what you send a journalist is both relevant to the publication and the subject/s the journalist covers on- and offline. With instant media coverage online, offering a story to a publication that recently covered the same subject is just silly unless your contribution is spectacularly different. However, online publications have lead times too. Some lead times are as long as for their print cousins – months.

The wired journalists are sometimes quite impatient with un-wired practitioners and are now becoming vocal about how they like to receive Internet based information. For example, if you send an e-mail or press release to one person at a publication, don't assume that it reaches everyone at, or associated with, the publication. That's especially true of the freelance members of the staff. (Contributor, special correspondent, contributing editor, senior contributing editor usually mean 'a freelance'.)

Even with the full-time staff of big magazines, journalists often do not talk to each other for days at a stretch. Some journalists are also competitive and do not disclose information to colleagues. Many work remotely and seldom go to the office. This means you do need a good relationship with news, features, product or specialist writers on each of the major publications.

The nature of online publishing is such that it often has immediate deadlines. Once a story has been written it can appear very quickly – or weeks later. These publications compete and as a result like to scoop each other. It is sensible to tailor stories so that each publication has a unique angle. The stories that are spiked are the me-too ones and the ones that have been scattered to every e-zine in the world.

Your release

There are some important new rules about your releases.

Rule one is to keep it short! Don't e-mail a press release that would print out to several pages. You need just enough so the journalist can decide whether or not he or she is interested.

As you will know from personal experience, dating any information is very important so always date your press release both in e-mail and in your virtual press office. Most journalists will not use material that is not dated (is this news or history?)

If you have a lot of information put it on a Web site and include the URL in your press release. Pages of detailed information can be organized and presented much better on a Web site than in an e-mail. If the journalist wants the information, he or she can visit your site, and a Web presentation would probably serve better than scrolling through a long e-mail.

As for the print media, when you send a news release to a major daily it's seldom going to be used in that form. Press releases aren't news, they carry news. So your goal in sending a release to a major newspaper is not to see the release used. There are a number of things you should be hoping for:

- your release makes an editor or reporter aware of your business, service, product or company and thereafter the next release will reinforce this;
- something in your release sparks an idea for a story and that you are used as a source;
- something in your release runs into a story currently in the planning stages and is used as a source.

This does not mean that you should not present copy that cannot be 'lifted' as is. The ability to 'cut and paste' words is as useful to a journalist as it is to you!

Newsrooms are different to features and other departments in a publication. There tends to be a person with responsibility to scan releases as they come in. In some news organizations this is done by the editor (or section editor) who flags the ones he or she finds interesting and passes them to the relevant reporter. In others it's done by a copy taster who then passes his or her selection to a more senior staff member. In either case, releases are read and some are sent into the news stream.

Being pithy and to the point is as important using e-mail as for print. Also, it's far easier to delete a message that isn't of interest than to look at and throw away a physical press pack that's off target. If the subject you provide to a publication is appealing, you need to be able to e-mail any additional information back to the journalist fast for two reasons. First, the story is up on his or her desktop and second, a long delay will mean your e-mail will be lost among hundreds of others from PR industry colleagues.

Using e-mail

E-mail is the preferred form for initial contact via the Internet.

Journalists using the Internet receive a lot of mail. They are in receipt of traditional press releases and press packs on paper, in faxes and via e-mails – thousands of them from all over the world. It is not unusual for a specialist technical journalist to receive between 50 and 100 unsolicited e-mails a day (one very five minutes)! As long as the information being sent is relevant to the specific subjects covered by that journalist and is original and important, he or she is happy to receive it.

Most journalists have now worked out that their e-mail system will allow them to automatically divert e-mails to a directory. Journalists will not 'see' the e-mail until they want to. They can, however, search all their e-mails against keywords, using their mail manager (such as Microsoft's Outlook).

In principle, journalists are not keen on attachments (to start with its harder to search attachments than copy in an e-mail). Word file attachments are ok for some, as long as they're not large. Some journalists will not open them because MS Word attachments contain the majority of all macro viruses. Ask before sending an attachment.

Images and PowerPoint attachments are not popular unless asked for. Many journalists work from a laptop. They often collect e-mails 'on the road' or at home, whichs means that they may have limited available disk space and slow links. A big attachment can take an age to download, might contain a virus and is very unfriendly to journalists.

A SUMMARY OF DOS AND DON'TS

- please use meaningful subject headers. And don't use subject headers that look like spam – anything with repeated exclamation marks, £ signs or all caps;
- do use a signature file with your full contact information (name, organization, address, telephone number/s, e-mail address and Web site/s);
- don't send a press release to your entire press list, with the entire recipient list visible. The reaction will tend to be: 'Well, someone else will be covering this if it's worth attention. I won't bother, because my article won't be unique.' Journalists like to feel special, even if they know otherwise;
- do turn off the option in your mail program that sends a second, HTML copy of the message as an attachment;
- don't attach an (electronic address) vCard.

The day of the embargo is gone. Not for publication until 00:00 hours can mean almost anything when the journalist may be half-way round the world. The better convention is to send a notice that an important story is to be issued by you on a certain date. Then the journalist can watch for it. Embargoes are a contract. Asserting one unilaterally is impossible.

There are some journalists who still use typewriters and many who still rely on fax, but the ones that really count use what is best to get a quality job done. This means that fax is, effectively, dead. If you must fax you have to tell the journalist. Most have to walk to the accounts department to find a working fax machine.

The phone

You should not call to find out if a journalist received your e-mailed press release. Among the 100 or so e-mails there has to be a great reason for such a call and the subject bar should have made that clear right from the beginning. Many writers work at home. While this used to be true mostly of freelance writers, it's just as true for magazine staff, nowadays. That makes the 'don't call' rule especially important.

Follow-ups are part of many PR organizations' normal operating procedure, but in many cases it's more likely to create resentment. It is appropriate to follow up on requested information, such as a sent press kit or product, but not on a blind mailing. If journalists are interested, and you subject line and copy are the stuff of media coverage, they will call or e-mail you.

When calling a journalist, be specific and don't assume that you are recognized or your story has been seen. This means you do need to say, 'I am calling from XX company about its forthcoming launch of YY product.' Give all the facts in the first sentence and, as for print journalists, never call a reporter on deadline day.

Don't use voice-mail as a substitute for e-mail and if you make a telephone call and can't make your point quickly, hang up. These days you can use e-mail instead.

If there's something that requires a journalist's attention in the e-mail, and he or she does not respond appropriately, a telephone call is appropriate if the story is significant. Most journalists are not so busy that they want to miss a scoop.

Conference calls

When journalists do request a conference call, you should be as unintrusive as possible. Personal, direct and interactive communication is now very easy and not very expensive, and conference calls can be made from your desktop.

The Internet allows journalist to write from anywhere. It makes the use of freelances even easier and media listings cannot always be relied on to accurately maintain the publication's interests, locations and addresses of journalists. It is always important to check where to send information and where to meet.

Previews

As for the printed media, don't ask to see an article you've helped a writer research before it appears in the publication. When you think about it, the writer should not show it to you because, first, his or her contract is with the journal and second, once submitted, it is the responsibility of an editor at the publication. In addition, it is the writer's responsibility to get the story right and he or she cannot share the responsibility by asking you to take some of it.

Staffers and freelances

You will have a number of journalists on your mailing list. Most like to be contacted when you have relevant information. But they also like to be able to tell you to take them off your mailing list if they do no think your material is relevant. Provide them with that facility. It saves both of you time and angst.

Although you may have your eye on the top magazine editors, you should really go out of your way to create a relationship with the freelances and staff writers who write about products relevant to your subject matter. They tend to be very expert and are the people who do the actual work.

It is a fact of life that there is a growing corps of freelances writing for both online and offline publications. This is one of the advantages of the Internet. But, as a result there will be occasions when freelances will approach you and you won't know who they are. It is right to be wary. It comes as a bit of a surprise to discover freelances do not visit their editor's office at all (not even for the Christmas bash). To be comfortable with a freelance, use a search engine to look at his or her work. It's reasonable to ask for an e-mail address and to look at his or her Web pages. If in doubt, politely ask the freelance if you can check with the editor for an assurance that this is a bona fide assignment.

Treat a freelance writer from a tiny publication with the respect you give the industry leading journalists. In three years, that freelance might become an editor at a top-flight publication, and will remember the people who treated him or her well.

Freelances make money only when they successfully pitch a story or review idea to an editor. It's tough, but then they also have lots more publications to pitch to and can use the online marts to find editors.

Different sections of a magazine will go at a topic from different perspectives and, as a PR person, you don't know what is happening in the editorial office, so be helpful to all journalists. Online publications can be vast and cover stories in a variety of ways.

Don't assume that news reporters will sign non-disclosure agreements. Some publications expressly forbid this. You waste your time when you book a meeting and don't bother to tell the journalist that it's under a non-disclosure agreement beforehand. There are quite a lot of journalists in the IT sector who are now saying that such agreeemnts have had their day. This suggests to me that the 'product launch' is on its way back but that now it will be a virtual event and very content rich.

INFORMATION YOU NEED ABOUT JOURNALISTS

The information you need about journalists has to be much more detailed these days. Some of the information you can assemble and place in your database includes the basics such as: name, addresses, phone, e-mail, instant messaging and, of course, work times and global time zones. For an individual story you may need to know deadlines and the full range of online and offline publications (even their own Web sites) where they contribute information.

Good media relations practices are important, which means you will know journalists' specific subject interests (held in a searchable list of 'keywords' and phrases) and the type of 'copy' they like to accept (news, features, backgrounders, white papers, hyperlinks (and what to), photo stories, sound and video.

Other facts you should gather include their preferred methods for communication (for initial contact, downloads – such as attachments); records of articles published; work rate (how many articles per week, month) and the news refresh cycles of their online and offline publications.

And now you have all this info, you need to work out how to use it effectively.

Journalists can now ask questions

Internet mailing lists for journalists provide a forum where they can seek specific news from Internet-connected PR practitioners and the publicity industry on a daily basis, resulting in a huge number of stories regularly placed on media outlets. You can also follow some of the discussions between journalists in discussion lists to find out their likes and dislikes.

Few clients really want respected journals to give them a dismissive press. One of the sure ways of attracting such rhubarb is through the practice of hyping a story. The Internet makes for transparency and a lot of Internet information shows clear provenance. For example, on your a Web site, important information, press releases and backgrounders will all be dated. A response that does not ring true becomes transparently dubious very quickly. Hype is exposed and spin is open to deep investigation by both online journalists and a much wider and sometimes very well-informed public.

A story sent to an online journalist can be researched in considerable depth very quickly. Your Web site is not the only one with facts about your story. The sites of competitors, industry associations, research companies, universities and keen enthusiasts all provide excellent added copy for the inquisitive journalist.

The opportunity to provide the bare facts in an e-mail press release and then to offer more detailed information via a Web site (which can be visible on your site or just put up for a short time to provide an added backgrounder and not immediately available to any but the most ardent surfer) is a boon.

MEASURING YOUR MEDIA RELATIONS EFFECTIVENESS

Media relations departments depend on journalist relationships to be successful. The cost of finding the right journalist is very high. The cost of losing one is even higher. With the numbers of journalists on your lists growing to meet the demands of the Internet, you need to be able to manage the cost of acquisition, maintenance and contact against the benefits you receive.

Evaluating you relationships with journalists is part of the job. You may like to check out what percentage of journalists on your database have used your releases each year and what percentage have not! Do you know the top three reasons journalists do not use your releases? It would be very useful to know and so would a reporting structure about your calls to journalists that don't use your material.

Most press relations practitioners should know what the lifetime value of journalists contact are. It is, after all, a measure of their worth and so is information such as how much it costs to find them initially. The powerful effect of personalized content for them will become self-evident with this information, as will the cost of sending them a releases and the cost of sending something that is irrelevant.

Do you know how much is costs to call them in a year (including time)? It's important to know the value you get from this investment and, with such information, you can become much more cost-effective. Is this a reason for you and your organization or an agency to have written journalist service quality standards? And do you or your company and agency articulate your media service quality standards in understandable and measurable terms to colleagues and journalists?

This means that the amount of content that you can make available and the extra and added references and cross-links that can provide enhanced richness for a journalist are well beyond even the most elaborate press pack. As long as the content is well written, to the point and relevant, the opportunities are endless.

Journalists, typically, do not have a lot of time to spare browsing slow sites. Elaborate design and flashy gizmos can be counter-productive (unless they add useful content for the journalist or his or her readers). This is a great opportunity to gain competitive advantage.

INTERNET 'MEDIA' LISTS, SPAM AND JAM

There is a mass of online outlets for news and information, and the practitioner needs to have a list of outlets for journalists using the Internet just as for the printed press release.

The problem is that whereas there a few thousand print publications for any single market, there are tens of thousands of online news outlets across the Internet. Its global nature means that the *Washington Post* is now important to an online audience in Germany.

A story can have an online journalist list running into thousands. In addition the capability to send a release to them all is simple – send an e-mail. The cost of sending one e-mail is akin to sending thousands! It's a no-cost, high-reach opportunity. The process is so simple that the temptation is almost irresistible and quickly becomes counterproductive. Part of the temptation is that clients are beginning to look for more content to appear about their organizations across the Internet. It is supposed to 'drive traffic to their Web site'.

Journalists and opinion formers using the Internet are not good intermediaries unless the information given to them is highly targeted or opens up opportunities for them. They are very resistant to spam (unsolicited e-mail) and jam (off-target and off-subject e-mailed news releases – or at it is referred to in the United States, off-beat e-mails).

Because the journalists are in control of the means for distribution, they can quite easily block e-mails from over-eager press agents and, using the Internet, can give a practitioner a very bad name very quickly. It is better to be able to service the actual needs of 20 journalists with good copy and effective communications tools than spam 100 journalists and upset most of them.

Such is the circulation of news, discussed elsewhere in this book, that good stories can have a significant circulation beyond the publications and e-zines where they are first published. Good stories in 20 publications will have a long life and wide circulation throughout the online media and in secondary circulation in other Web sites and discussion lists. In addition, virtual news feeds provide copy for old media as well. Already, for some journalists in the printed sector, a quarter of the content of their stories comes from the Internet.

The important concept to bear in mind is that quality and focus pay the best dividends. In addition, there is a need to re-examine the nature of the media. The online magazines run by Tesco's and IBM are very important and have a role to play alongside Silicon.com, Reuters and the *Basingstoke Gazette*.

There are other outlets for your press releases. There are a number of commercial, academic, government, trade and professional Web sites that have a need for original news and copy. A Chamber of Commerce site may welcome pages prepared by you (but that look like part of its site) and thus the number and range of outlets is significantly larger than first thought.

As long as the active, aware and latent publics and the issues and topic-led Internet constituents are evident, there is an opportunity to provide copy for the outlets they use. News on the Net creates a buzz and it is available to the practitioner who cares to seek the best opportunities.

YOUR VIRTUAL PRESS OFFICE

One of the burning issues for many practitioners is the form and nature of their online press facility. This facility is a Web site in its own right. This may be an integral site within the main Web site or hosted (but branded in the style of the organization) by an agent or consultant, branding being very important to online presence.

Most of the content needed is common sense. The basic idea is to look at your virtual press office from the perspective of the journalist.

A journalist's facility

As with all other Internet interaction, the visitor has choices. Journalists can choose not to use your site.

In researching journalists' opinion for this book, one front-page editor said that he regularly had to scratch stories because it took too long to verify information from corporate Web sites' press facilities. Ten minutes finding the relevant information is an eternity as deadlines approach.

Imagine the journalists visiting your virtual press office. With 150 e-mails, a phone call on average every 11 minutes, nearly an hour's work opening the post and even in these days, faxes, a journalist can be very busy. From all this input, he or she may have to research and write two to four stories. This is a busy schedule even without internal and external meetings, launches and events to attend. There may also be sub-editing and, for some, layout, proofing and passing pages depending on the kind of publication. So the journalist visiting your virtual news centre is short of time - and wants to get to the bacon and get out. The journalist will also want to enjoy the experience. An ideal facility is described below.

It is easy to find the virtual press office both from the organization's Web site and from the PR consultant's site. Just one click, fast download and there, laid out on the desktop, are the recent headlines each dated and with a two-line synopsis. There is also a symbol showing what is corporate news, financial news, product news, a case study, survey, white paper, etc.

The headline gives the facts with no frills, a date line (time, date and where from). The story has a first sentence with the facts and a short first paragraph with the meat. At this point the journalist can opt to continue or look elsewhere. Because the process was straightforward, the visit will be appreciated.

All too many virtual press centres waste time, stories are puffs and the construction of press releases is rambling. The corporate-speak in online press releases is a natural breeding ground for cynical reporting. On a Web site, they pretty well ensure there will be no repeat visits except for very prejudiced reporting in the alternative online media. Some of the biggest corporations in the world churn out this nonsense and are then surprised to be targeted at the World Economic Forum for being remote from real people. They should visit their online pressroom.

Copy plus

Having passed the first hurdle, the story page will have copy that does not take up the full width of the page. There is a lot of associated material and hyperlinks alongside the text too (but not embedded in the text which makes 'cut and paste' difficult).

There is a link to associated pictures and graphics. A quick look reveals thumbs (small pictures) which, when clicked on, enlarge if needed to see details. Theses pictures can be downloaded as JPG, TIFF, or GIF for Web, PC or Mac publishing and there is an option of 75 dpi, 300 dpi, or 1200 dpi for Web publishing, newsprint, small size reproduction or a full front page for a glossy magazine. There is also a direct hyperlink to these pictures with cut and paste HTML code. This means that the pictures can be embedded in an online journal from your virtual press office – no downloading needed. The photos have factual captions, date taken and copyright release to bona fide media prepared to provide quickly entered information such as publication, circulation/repeat site visits and journalists' e-mail.

There is also an option to use AVI or Realplayer video or sound files. There are 56k, ADSL, ISDN or T1 connection options. There is a short introduction about each and a drop-down menu to allow a direct link (cut and paste HTML code). There is an option to download Web cast and TV quality sound and radio clips. Copyright is released with the same proviso as above.

The release has contact details to the PR practitioner giving a name and options of address, phone, e-mail, instant messaging and a clock to identify times available for direct contact from most major cities in the world (remember, the Internet is global). In a big press office it will be important to have backgrounders about press officers and their respective responsibilities. Most journalists have difficulty in separating the company spokesperson from the press officer, PR manager, corporate affairs managers, director of reputation management, investor relations executive and community affairs coordinator. So do I.

Links from press releases

From a link on the press release, there are expert or executive commentators giving short biographical notes and the direct contact details plus added backgrounders, white papers, survey results, added external Internet resources for research purposes, comparison data (with personal commentary) giving more detail about the press release's subject matter.

A further and key benefit are the hyperlinks that point to real-time, sector-specific news at sites such as AP, Reuters, PRnewswire, FT.com, BBC, CNN, etc, and a number of other trusted news sources (the newsworthiness of these sites may be enhanced by streamed or updated content in a side bar). These links offer direct contact to current and related news and background media reporting from round the world. This means that there is a quick way to add current content and richness to the story. Real-time news giving currency for, say, a three-month-old case study, can make it very attractive and a great source for story ideas. The facility provided to the journalist means that, without having to search elsewhere on the Web, all the facts are present to turn a press release into powerful copy. From the release the journalist can also elect to view, cut and copy, with options to paste copy with or without embedded hyperlinks.

To add that extra line of copy and access it fast, each press release page will have a search capability and options to search the virtual press office, story links and the organization's full Web sites by keyword and by using Boolean logic. Links to your related news and stories in the virtual pressroom are also provided.

A number of facilities are also provided including the means for assembling (writing) the story at the site and then downloading it or forwarding it direct to third parties such as the editor. A similar facility is available for big files that take time to download – such as pictures, video and sound files.

There is an opt-in capability that allows the journalist to elect to receive information from the organization. The journalists can elect to receive short headers plus a URL link to stories as e-mail alerts, e-mails with text stories and an 'opt-in' choice of subject matter such as corporate, financial, product, launch, case study, white papers and product. A further option is to be included on your 'buddy lists' so that facts can be ascertained in real time as the story is being written. This is when the journalist is asked to disclose more information such as his or her name, and which other publications he or she writes for (many journalists write for several titles) and, in particular, his or her specific professional interests. It is only a tiny step thereafter for your virtual press office to welcome the journalist at the next visit: 'Hello June, welcome back, you may be especially interested in this story about...'. A personal and warming welcome – who could resist?

From within this press release page, the reporter can take the story, add rich and up-to-date content, news, expert opinion from the organization and independent third party fact and expertise. In a very short time a journalist can have a well researched, thoroughly endorsed and up-to-the-minute article with all the graphical information needed for a news story, a full-blown feature article or TV documentary. With so much valuable stuff, the journalist might also sign up for the press office e-mail newsletter and automatic updated and 'pushed' new stories.

Your organization will also have the stickiest virtual press office in the world, meaning that journalists will want to come to your site because there will always be a story or story idea that can be sparked from any of your press releases and they will always have that essential element of newsworthiness.

So much for the journalist's visit to your virtual press office.

The practitioner activity

All these facilities will concern practitioners for two reasons.

The first is the apparent loss of control: the loss of direct contact with the journalist and uncertainty as to who is taking information from the virtual press office. The second is the other people in the organization who will be in direct contact with the media and not through the press office. It's a nightmare.

Learn to live with it and make sure that the whole organization lives with it too. The case for protecting the media Web pages (also called 'virtual press office', 'media centre', 'news' and lots of other less helpful titles) from the prying eyes of the public is pretty slim, but there is some justification.

Thousands of people accessing your site and trying to download a picture from your server can simply bring the whole site to a standstill. In some cases there is material by academics and experts that is for background briefing and which has copyright restriction, and occasionally there is deep background you want to make available to commentators prior to 'the big event'. These are all good reasons for having part of your online virtual press office password protected. This does not mean that the information is in any way privileged. If your competitors want the information, they can get it.

If you have special information, have separate Web sites, even a separate virtual press office or other resource. There are occasions for creating Web pages that are not easily identified on the Internet. Train internal people and keep them informed and then train them again.

The journalist has access to the information anyway. Journalists can search the Internet; journalists can e-mail your head of research or CEO direct. Government and universities, consumer groups and the rest are already online and offer a lot of free information. By offering direct contact, it is possible to manage the level of interest and time a journalist will spend on a site and in working on the organization's story. In addition, accurate background briefing and biographical details are provided, a facility not available when the process is ad hoc and driven by the journalists. From information completely beyond the control of the practitioner, an open and informative virtual press office provides focus that favours the organization.

The benefit for the journalists is speed and comprehensive information. The benefit for the practitioner is accuracy, content and, above all, coverage.

The other concern is the amount of work needed for every press release. Such is the transparency and porosity of the organization and all the other influences on a story, that making life difficult for the journalist, or not offering every facility to the journalist, will simply mean he or she will go elsewhere and especially to the competitor who offers good facilities.

Another concern is the amount of work that seems to be involved in providing such extensive facilities. Absolutely wrong. Most of these apparent added facilities require simple online Web-based forms to be completed. The parts that are difficult to automate are research, establishment of reliable third party sources and writing copy and captions. Embedding URLs offering options of graphic formats, providing HTML code and all those apparently sophisticated computing activities are automated, even down to archiving.

More sophisticated virtual press offices will require high levels of skills and processes, but the routines required are not difficult. The essential job of taking the brief, writing, gaining approvals, assembling online resources and building lists are dealt with in this book. This does mean that there have to be standardized internal procedures and management of the processes designed to allow flexibility. But even these are largely automatable and certainly take less time than old-fashioned practices. The hardest part will be serving the needs of journalists who are not Internet savvy. Fortunately – a dying breed.

As with all online relationships, monitoring the activity you engender has many benefits. For example, do your press releases provoke an increase in Web site visits? Do reporters ask for information and do they ask to be added to or taken off your circulations list, and to what extent is your Web site an effective resource for the media?

Whatever the resources you offer in a virtual press office, there are three overriding needs. Contact details on every page and every release, good navigation and short download times. If it takes 10 seconds to get past the organization's front page before a journalist can click on the 'press office' link, he or she is lost to you. Remember the saying: 'Hurry up – I haven't got all minute.'

17

Issues management

Practitioners will face issues that are largely driven by Internet activity. The distinction between online and offline issues or issues management is rapidly becoming blurred. Here we deal with the online elements.

The objective for the practitioner is not necessarily to eliminate the presence of particular issues among 100 million people or more who are connected at any one time to the Internet, but to change them to be mutually advantageous for the constituency and the organization. In some rare cases, this means that the issue will go away. As in every walk of life, well-managed issues fade and eventually die or are buried in half-remembered folklore.

How information is served up to the Internet audience is now significant. Not only is this important for the development of richness and reach, it is significant in the formation of a constituency relationship. By knowing the issues relevant to constituents, and who those constituents are, the organization is able both to find out why there is an attraction between the company and the person or people involved and why the relationship has been formed.

The process will follow some quite well-rehearsed routines such as identify the issue for the organization (see Chapter 12) and its perceived constituents.

Identification of existing active, aware, latent constituents and offline publics is dealt with in Chapter 9 as is access to, collation and application of knowledge acquired by and from constituents and offline sources, the corporate intranet and the Internet. Such information is vital for all issues management and if it is routinely maintained will be ready and useful for issues management.

Issues management, with the information available from the processes identified above, can quickly move towards development of concepts for response (online and/or offline). On the other hand, without some very effective assessment of the nature of the online constituents, response development can be just downright dangerous.

The response you develop will include details of required processes on- and offline and an assessment of the concept for:

- consequential transparency;
- consequential agency;
- consequential porosity.

As with all Internet activities, practitioners should look to a return on capital and, just to make sure there are no reputation-wrecking glitches in your response, you will always trial the solution before you implement the programme and monitor and evaluate the results.

ISSUES

Issues can be both helpful and unhelpful for a company. Helpful issues may be that the constituents recognize that they want information before making a buying decision. By helping the constituent to resolve the issue, the company will gain a customer. Other issues are not so benign. The process for management is largely the same.

Broadly paraphrasing Professor Grunig, issues have three characteristics that affect how publics react: problem recognition, constraint recognition and level of involvement:[1]

---

[1] Grunig, J and Hunt, T (1994) *Public Relations Techniques*, Holt, Rinehart and Winston, New York

- In *recognizing* a problem people will actively seek information about the issue that concerns them and/or record (or *process*) information that comes to them unsought.
- *Constraint* recognition describes the extent to which people believe there are obstacles that limit their ability to fulfil their plans.
- *Involvement* means the extent to which a person feels connected to a particular situation and will determine whether he or she is likely to *act* or not.

Analysis of Web sites and newsgroup content provides constant and up-to-date issues management information. The analysis tools that are now available from evaluation companies and content analysis software, make these processes very simple and inexpensive. In looking at your online (and offline) content you can ask:

- Are these people seeking information?
- Are people saying they can't get information?
- Are people doing things (or saying they are doing things)?

If the answer is yes, you have an issue.

Interaction

Having identified issues and related publics, the concept for response needs to be considered.

Because there are so many forms of communication across the Internet, and the conventions can be different even between one newsgroup or Web site and the next, agreed processes do need to be developed and can be applied using a flowchart such as the example shown in Figure 17.1.

'ROGUE' SITES

People set up Web sites for a range of reasons. Some do so with the aim of damaging the reputation of organizations. The agenda for some is even more dangerous, and they have come to be known generically as 'rogue sites'.

Internet surfers easily find rogue sites. The authors of such sites

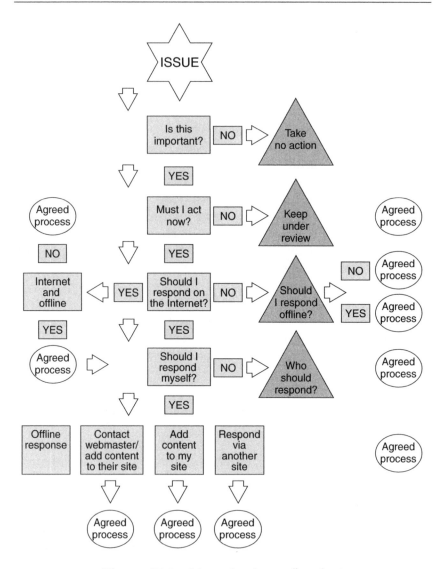

Figure 17.1 *Managing issues flowchart*

are not particularly accountable for what they (or their contributors) write. They are not held to any sort of journalistic standard. They are using the facility of the Internet to express an opinion, garner support, parody, criticize, or argue their case against organizations.

They can be shrugged off as disaffected cranks, a confused

minority or unfortunates, but that would be to dismiss them too easily. They have the potential to reach a mass international audience which can be fascinated, entertained or easily led into believing half-truths as fact or ranting as a legitimate concern. In addition, these sites can address legitimate concerns, highlight real failings or expose shortcomings that need redress.

In some instances they offer an opportunity for companies and consumers to re-evaluate their position and enhance their activities. Certainly, such sites can and will distract managers. Rogue sites cannot be ignored. They need to be managed.

Experience shows us that a number of traditional remedies for disaffected critics are not nearly as effective online. The use of the law in a blaze of Internet criticism, 'buying off' perpetrators and putting pressure on third parties such as ISPs, tend to be, at best, a short-term remedy. The McSpotlight and Untied Airlines case studies are classic examples of how dramatically, and expensively, such activities can backfire. In both cases these big organizations won battles and have, to date, lost the online war.

The appearance of a Web site created by the McDonald's activists came in February 1996 when Morris and Steel launched the McSpotlight Internet site from a laptop connected to the Internet via a mobile phone outside a McDonald's store in Central London. The Web site was accessed more than a million times in its first month. It was headline news across the world. By any standards, the McSpotlight site is big and has an amazing amount of content. A large part of the content is critical of McDonald's and some is allegedly libellous.

On 19 June 1997, after a case said to have cost the company over £10 million and a £60,000 settlement against Morris and Steel, the Web site was accessed 2.2 million times. The first paradox is that McDonald's won the court case but the allegations are still on the Web site and available to this day (and is mirrored across the world so that if it is turned off in one country, its content can be accessed from another).

The second paradox is that with so much criticism about the company available for all to see, it remains one of the most successful food retailers across the world. McDonald's is the largest and best-known global foodservice retailer with more than 24,500 restaurants in 116 countries. Its share price is four times higher than when the McSpotlight site was launched and dividends per share are up 44 per cent.

Is there a linkage between corporate performance and Internet criticism? Is it possible to overreact?

ROGUE SITES

A good case study and links to examples of rogue sites is available at: http://www.cyberalert.com/whitepaper.html.

There is no question that a number of stakeholders can be readily unnerved by Internet activism. In addition, because they have a direct interest in the organization under scrutiny, they tend to be more directly involved and affected.

Monitoring the Internet is essential for a number of reasons and identification of rogue sites is one. Of course, many companies (most of the big ones) have at least one rogue site. These are Web sites with the single purpose of denigrating an organization or person. The objective may, at worst, be aimed at pulling the organization down. When they are well executed these sites hurt and certainly someone's pride will be pricked. Anger and emotional outbursts tend to cloud judgement and are counter productive.

Managing rogue sites

When a rogue site is discovered, one of the most important things to do is to say nothing, but start monitoring immediately and work through your checklist of necessary actions.

ROGUE SITE CHECKLIST

- Research and evaluate the site or sites that are causing concern.
- Apply the evaluation processes.
- Think and strategize.
- Act ethically.
- Take the high ground.
- Turn disadvantage into opportunity.
- Lock up spin-doctors.
- Put lawyers on a very short leash.
- Act.

This will create an opportunity to focus on professional management. The processes can be rehearsed (especially with senior managers), which will make the whole experience much less harrowing all round. Instant, unconsidered and ill-informed knee-jerk reaction will, almost inevitably, be damaging.

Each eventuality will be different, but the elements of the checklist and the consequential management can be established to allow the practitioner to develop strategies in advance of the inevitable call from someone who has found a site.

The best recommendation this book can make is to have a process planned now even if you do not believe you have been or will ever be affected by a rogue site.

PLANNING IN ADVANCE

- Assemble your case, then work through scenarios and consequences.
- Identify the opportunities for enhanced transparency. (Is this a time to expose broader management thinking and/or a wider range of facts? Is it possible to roll out transparency progressively, enlist trade associations, publish research?)
- Always take the high ground. (For example ensure the site owner and the wider public have relevant facts that will push the onus of proof and validation back to the site owner.)
- Is an action going to box you in?
- Is the site gaining overwhelming support? Is your current position indefensible requiring tactical withdrawal, regrouping and then response?
- Are there ways you can devote limited resources to respond but keep extra resources in reserve?
- Can you divide your response and engage the site in different ways (logical argument, fact files, engage the sites' constituents in another way, bring third party influence to bear)?
- Gauge your response, timing, force, and tactical application.
- Change internal working practices or enhance relevant activities, learn lessons.

Pressure that has dangers

Confrontation is bad news. It becomes an undignified brawl between you – Goliath and him – David.

Where there is no escape for the site owner, he or she will defend to the death – and at enormous cost to your reputation. Some considerations do need extra relationship management before a company acts. Where there is libel, the solution is often better dealt with using arbitration, but if you can sue, would you find it beneficial to do so after you have taken into account transparency, porosity and Internet agency considerations? If you sue will your reputation suffer in court and do you know who you will sue? In cyberspace this can be problematic. Of course, before you even begin, you will want to ensure that your lawyer is Internet savvy.

Sometimes the solution is as simple as an approach to an ISP (but not always). Some ISPs may be worried about the content and may pull the site, but if the ISP/host pulls the site will it appear elsewhere – or a similar or morphed version?

There are arguments for using the courts, applying pressure to ISPs, and in some instances the use of policemen. Such remedies must not be dismissed out of hand just because we live in a so-called transparent era.

Newsgroups

Does the site owner moderate the newsgroup? Is it unmoderated and is the site enthusiast open to persuasion? Is there potential for insensitive responses? Is there time to get to know the newsgroup's culture? Be very careful.

Lots of organization are put off by the possibility that they can get themselves into deep water by participating in newsgroups and discussion lists. They can, but it's not nearly as awesome as many make out. The biggest issue is the fantastic amount of time that can be wasted in the process.

It is important to lurk and to make sure you have a planned response. You will need to be prepared to be flexible and you need to use appropriate and ready-made processes. Of course, you have to be sure you can respond across a range of channels (Web, newsgroups and bulletin boards, press, radio and television, government regulators, globally) and can respond from a number of angles and through a variety of channels if needed.

Do not pretend to be anyone other than yourself and use the expertise and strengths of your organization. As always use facts without spin and expert opinion, and why not use the facilities of the Internet to aid your cause?

Simply killing off a site may just leave burning resentment and an inevitable, and expensive rerun. Your objective is not to eliminate the site, your objective is to turn the disadvantage into an opportunity.

THE IMPOSSIBLE ATTACK

In March 1997, the well-known US fashion designer, Tommy Hilfiger, was accused of making racist remarks during an appearance on *The Oprah Winfrey Show*. Tommy Hilfiger denies ever making such remarks. Both he and spokespeople for Ms Winfrey maintain he has neither appeared nor been asked to appear on *The Oprah Winfrey Show*. This did not prevent a mass of comment in dozens of newsgroups pointing at Tommy Hilfiger and branding him as a racist.

Even the most exhaustive PR campaigns cannot easily refute rogue information allowed to spread too long. In spite of well-publicized responses the newsgroup talk online disparages Tommy Hilfiger's supposed remarks to this day.

Even in the face of undeniable fact, some people just do not want to believe a truth that contradicts their view. There are lots of people like that in cyberspace and, because it is universal, big and global and can reach out to the world, these people have a more powerful say than they deserve.

The key for everyone is to find disparaging comments early and to put the record straight. This has the merit of containing an unwarranted outburst. There is little to commend inaction.

Organizations that are susceptible to protracted attack with no basis for truth might investigate why they should be the subject of such attention. Paying close attention to the motivation of critics, however hard a pill this may be to swallow, could yield reputation-enhancing intelligence.

18

What is right and legal

If a newspaper as respected as the *Sunday Times* can make a copyright mistake (see Chapter 16), then it comes as little surprise to discover that such infringements are common and frequent and extend well beyond the realm of newspapers.

The law applies online as much as offline. Its application can be muddied because of the differences in legal systems and between the laws of different countries. Innocence of the law is no protection against prosecution and until a range of anomalies is cleared up, practitioners need to be wary of breaking the law and alert to those who would offend against their organizations.

The Internet will, in time, force new laws upon many of us and copyright will be one set of laws that will change quite radically. This means that the practitioner has to be aware of what is and is not legal in different territories and countries. Now that you are providing information globally (and there is very little PR that, today, is not global) you need to be careful.

Because a lot of our communication goes from one computer to another via routers (and this can happen hundreds of times for a single package of information) and the Internet does not care which router is being used, your message can get to some strange places. Some of them have laws that allow governments, crooks and other people to look at the information passing through. This is particularly true of e-mail but can apply to other communications too. If your information breaks the local law, you could be held responsible. Now, most of your messages and Internet connection are so fragmented and are going via so many different routers that the information makes very little sense and is certainly part of a massive volume of data, so you would be very unlucky to be singled out.

At the next level, of course, there are governments, like in the UK, that are trying to intercept Internet content. This does not really affect criminals but does affect the great bulk of commercial traffic. So information, innocently and legally provided to a third party but available to a snooping government (which can 'pull' information), can be inspected and, if it contravenes a local regulation, you or your organization can be held responsible.

So far, the law is not clear in many areas of Internet activity and there is a lot of work in progress. The responsible person can use common sense and, when necessary, international lawyers. There will be some major legal wrangles and many governments will try to enact rules that are simply not applicable to a network of networks.

The Internet is largely self-balancing. It is populated by citizens of the world who are mostly intelligent, law-abiding, friendly, upright and honest. Among other things, they do not tolerate uncivilized behaviour and, using the power of the Internet, regulate its abuse. That is not to say there is no need for rules or for governments to take part. It does mean that they need the consent of the Internet public.

As a practitioner, kicking over the traces of what is acceptable will bring retribution. If you spam your constituents, they will punish you. If you try to deceive, the Internet will reveal truths. If you pretend (in a realm of pretence) you will be exposed. It may happen today, next week or next month. And it isn't fair. Lots of people can be anonymous and many can deceive, but you have no choice if you want a long-term existence. You have to play straight by your Internet constituents.

In looking at the nature of Internet integrity, we might take heed of Professor Drucker:

> Organizations must competently perform the one social function for the sake of which they exist – the school to teach, the hospital to cure the sick, and the business to produce goods, services, or the capital to provide for the risks of the future. They can do so only if they single-mindedly concentrate on their specialized mission. But there is also society's need for these organizations to take social responsibility – to work on the problems and challenges of the community. Together these organizations are the community. The emergence of a strong, independent, capable social sector – neither public sector nor private sector – is thus a central need of the society of organizations. But by itself it is not enough – the organizations of both the public and the private sector must share in the work.[1]

On the one hand, Drucker proposes that the practitioner focuses on the activities of the organization and on the other he suggests that you take responsibility for the wider effects of your organization in and on society.

This does not mean that organizations have to be all things to all men. It does mean that your organization has to be capable of presenting and defending its principles and practices and, at the end, to be lawfully and socially acceptable for the work and achievements of its people. The reason this becomes important has been made clear in a number of cases where Internet communities have driven a wedge between government and organization and thereby empowered NGOs. The NGOs have won the day by winning the arguments, largely with online, global, constituents. In some instances winning the argument was wrong and they got away too lightly.

The assumption that business, especially big business, is bad is wrong, but until business defends itself, it will continue to lose the arguments. Its record of being weak and unwilling to engage with society at large is significant. There is a need to be part of the debate taking place between constituents.

COPYRIGHT

In the meantime there are some conventions in transition. Copyright is one of them. Copyright is a relatively modern idea and is not very happy as a convention in cyberspace. There will be

---

[1] Drucker, P F (1994) The age of social transformation, *The Atlantic Monthly*, November 1994

a different convention in time, but for now the law relating to the Internet is fraught with strange interpretations. It is a focus in this book because it affects practitioners in many ways.

Considerable guidance is available in the UK and there is a global resource that can also help the PR practitioner. The World Intellectual Property Organization (WIPO; (http://www. wipo.org/) is an intergovernmental organization with headquarters in Geneva, Switzerland. It is one of the 16 specialized agencies of the United Nations and is the global forum for matters of intellectual property issues.

The nature of copyright

Where a practitioner has any doubt on the matter of intellectual property, proper legal advice must be sought. The comments here are offered without prejudice and for guidance only.

Copyright has the characteristic of 'literary and artistic works'. It is understood to be original creations in the fields of literature and arts and can be expressed in words, symbols, music, pictures, three-dimensional objects, software or any combination.

The laws of a state relating to copyright cannot provide for the protection of the state's citizens in another state, but under the 1886 Berne Convention, the International Union for the Protection of Literary and Artistic Works, a number of countries have created comparable forms of protection for authors. This is reasonably helpful for Internet applications where precedent is created by Supreme Courts. In the meantime there is a lot of local precedent and local law that has not been tested.

The essential rules of copyright apply to Internet-related activities. While this may be confusing because of the global nature of the Internet in which different nations have differing cultural and legal rules, the essential truth is that original work belongs to the person who created it unless it is created specifically for a third party in whom, under such circumstances, the copyright will rest.

If the law were that easy, life would be simple. It is not. But as a guiding principle, the concept of copyright and associated protection of intellectual properties and a range of processes must be considered protected, both having been enshrined in law and reinforced by judicial precedent.

While these laws were invented in recent times, are culturally unacceptable to a large proportion of the world's population and are unsuited to a large part of the practice and culture of the Internet, they are the law and must be upheld.

Using and giving copyright

Asking permission to use copyright is not hard and, for the most part, where copyright is withheld by one expert publishing on the Internet it will be granted by an equally respected but different source.

This will raise issues inside organizations. The culture of many companies and institutions is to protect and defend copyright and other intellectual properties. In doing so, it is not that such assets will not become available on the Internet to those who seek hard enough, it is that there will be a loss of opportunity to create relationships and transfer of advantage to a competitor. Each organization will want to create its own rules.

The guiding principle that may help is to identify where the real value lies. Information, while an asset in itself and, quite possibly a competitive advantage, may be the lesser value compared to the organization's capability to create original intellectual works or access to markets. Where the greater value lies in the capability to be original, creative and at the leading edge, there is considerable advantage in adding authority to your own organization's reputation through transparency.

Implications of using hyperlinks

When you link to another Web site or Web page, there are copyright implications. These come to the fore when you share your knowledge or send a reference to a Web site or Web page. There are two types of linking, deep linking and linking to copyrighted material, which have led to a spate of law cases. Let's take a look at the cases each spawned and the implications of each.

Deep linking

Deep linking, or linking to a page deep inside a Web site, bypasses the home page. This means that organizations' investment in time and money on content, navigation and interactive considerations is bypassed. The visitor will not see parts of the site which aid revenue generation (from 'click-through' agreements or banner advertisements, for example), terms and conditions, licence agreements or content that provides context for the site.

At the same time, the nature of the Web is openness; linking is an essential element in making the Web a powerful medium for communication, commerce, and discovery. This dichotomy has reached the courts in the United States and a recent judgement ruled that 'hyperlinking does not itself involve a violation of the (USA) Copyright Act' and, 'There is no deception in what is happening. This is analogous to using a library's card reference to particular items, albeit faster and more efficiently.' I concur but practitioners may want to make up their own minds on such an issue

The appropriate rule for practitioners is to ask permission from the site before adding it to your resource where others may use it in the name of your organization (for example on your Web site). Practitioners may like to consider how they will respond to deep linking. Certainly, your site should include a clause that you prefer to be asked and treat every application on merit.

There are disadvantages in allowing deep linking but many more advantages as long as your site is constructed with the possibility of this happening borne in mind.

Linking to intellectual properties

If your link is to copyright or propriety material, it could be that you are inciting a person to infringe copyright.

On the one hand, such a link could be construed as being similar to a footnote in a book. Alternatively, because of the speed and ease of linking, this can be considered a contribution to copyright infringement. Footnotes can be valid or not and the author will not be responsible if the information is inaccurate or proprietary information.

At present there is little guidance that applies universally. However, there appears to be a consensus that suggests that if hyperlinking is designed to or has the intent to incite violation of copyright or other intellectual properties, it is unacceptable, but not hyperlinking or identifying the Web page that has been linked to.

An international outlook

The thing we all find difficult is that we now operate in an international arena and yet we know so little of different cultures round the world.

Lending money in the West is acceptable but not in the Middle East. The value of the word of a Syrian is greater that a written contract. The urgency of action is not so significant throughout the world.

There are some underlying principles of humanity and community and, with the valuable assistance of the Internet, we can learn at first hand from the connected nations of the world how we can work in an acceptable framework with different people.

Falling into cultural and legal black holes has to be avoided because you or your organization can be sucked into events that take over from the proper running of your affairs.

19

And of the future

A lot of people are unsure about the extent to which this revolution will affect them and society. Um... they missed it. It is storming away ahead of them.

For years it seemed no one wanted to take much notice of the Internet and PR, but by the mid-1990s its significance was elevated to gold rush frenzy, first in the United States and four years later in Western Europe. The aftermath of the bursting dotcom bubble in the millennium year was that many people realized that most other people were connected to the Internet. Every organization needed a Web presence of some kind. At the same time, most people sagged under a blizzard of e-mail.

PR SITES

http://www.ipr.org.uk
http://www.prca.or.uk
http://www.prsource.co.uk/
http://www.prstudy.com/
http://www.instituteforpr.com
http://www.ipranet.org

---

http://www.prWebcast.com
http://www.ragan.com
http://www.xpresspress.com/
http://www.prnewswire.com/mediainsider
http://www.mediamap.com/
http://www.clickz.com/
http://publicrelations.about.com/careers/publicrelations/
http://www.wilsonWeb.com/Webmarket/pr.htm
http://www.prWeb.com
http://www.usprnet.com/

The City and financial gamblers managed to lose a lot of money and it seemed that we all returned to pre-Web normality. But we didn't. Everyone expected that everything would be available and supported online. The real bubble was still there. When visiting a theatre site we expect to find map for getting there, 10 minutes before we leave home (not to mention some nice local restaurants) and when such information is not available, our whole experience of the evening is spoiled. Today there are expectations that did not exist before the dotcoms emerged in the financial markets.

This kind of instant response has become a habit and gives us a glimpse of how life has changed. Every organization now has a Web site or is dying. Soon we will all need integrated relationships, but the distinction between being online or not will be so blurred that no one will be able to tell. The hype has gone – good riddance – the real revolution carries on.

It is important that PR practitioners should look to how their work is changing. One tiny example is the use of fax. Once it was the preferred method for much communication. Today, if it is used at all, it is via a PC just like another form of e-mail and no one knows which technology you are using. The time and cost involved in processing, sending and receiving faxes, once a main-stay of communication, disappeared in three years. What we have seen so far are the tiny foothills of the changes under way. These changes are all about communication and so are important, if not critical, to you.

There is the issue of the have-nots. The people who do not want to use the Internet seem to be missing so much. There are those people who cannot afford or do not want a PC and exorbitantly priced access to the network, and there are those who do not want to waste time gazing at an Internet-driven computer screen. There are those who are intimidated by the technology and the idea of using a keyboard and mouse. For people who worry about such matters there is great relief in knowing that the range of delivery options, now large but about to explode, will give everyone an opportunity to take part in the communications revolution on their own terms and to meet their specific needs.

EXAMPLES OF ONLINE PR RESPONSES TO MARKET NEED

http://www.imtstrategies.com/prstudy
http://www.eisite.com/services/site.html
http://www.netcurrents.com/report/sample.html
http://www.outrider.com/process/services_public_relations.html

---

The role of PR is to ensure that we have available the forms for communication and methodologies needed to build relationships. In the past we have, inadequately, used the media as our principle link. Today 'the media' is rapidly becoming a cipher for the Internet, which means we have to change pretty quickly.

Perhaps in a book to a predominantly creative profession, it is not too difficult to point to the future. A future when delivery of data can be as fast and as acceptable as real time conversations alongside pictures better than television or surround sound cinema. A future when the range of Internet delivery devices and the knowledge associated with them is germane, relevant and accessible.

There are five concurrent things to watch:

1. Information value added processes.
2. Many forms for transmission of information.
3. Technology integration.
4. New communication devices.
5. Ever more ways to communicate.

The mixture of information that is now available in cyberspace is already unimaginable. The numbers we use to describe its size are too big for us to actually conceive. Already, our ability to slice, dice, sort and reconstruct information using amazing computing power is available and, more important, very easy to understand, configure and apply. For example, there is very little software that the PR professional will use that takes more than three days to learn. Most can be learnt (maybe not perfectly) on the job. Managing the vast galactic Internet cloud of information is impossible, but creating a bright star like a beacon of knowledge or insight or enhanced quality of life is possible. The search, analysis and semiotic programs are powerful tools. The data-mining programs for CRM are really quite clever. The only constraint to creating and using the information available on the Internet is imagination.

Transmission of information, until now mostly via underground wires and fibre-optic cable, is increasingly by cellular telephony. But we are already seeing personal communications access via satellite and other more exotic forms for transferring information using sound as well as light.

There is the extra phenomenon of technologies joining together to integrate television signals and data down a telephone line to provide interactive television programmes. Meanwhile cell phone networks integrate with GPS (Global Positioning System) in cars to deliver relevant Internet-driven information about route planning and the nearest restaurant. The integrated cell phone messaging services offer the flexibility of e-mail on the move, pager and mobile conversation, all of which can also be accessed from your desktop.

To provide everyone with access to this information, a wider and growing range of delivery devices such as WAP phones and PDA pocket books are added to PCs and kiosks. The Internet-enabled cuddly toy offers bedtime stories delivered in a very friendly way to a child. This technological change means that information will be available to meet a specific need, but only when it is needed and selected by individual users.

This leads us to the range of communication that can be deployed. Sounds, vision, touch and smell can be manipulated by these technologies and their associated devices. They can be quite mundane in their delivery, such as an e-mailed press release for a journalist to look at. But it may be fun to attach a sound or a movement just to add extra interest and information. If the story is shocking enough... what about a shock as well? The technology is already waiting for you to use it.

These are the technical things. They have to be conquered at some level in order that the really clever ideas and applications can be appreciated. Only then can we access the real change and revolution. A whole world having such technology and communication at its fingertips releases enormous energy. The best of global knowledge is becoming available to the most talented people and the systems for ensuring connection are becoming more robust.

There was time when individual pieces of knowledge were like dust; gradually their own gravity brought them together. As in the creation of space and time, cyberspace has created itself and has no centre but gives birth to galaxies and solar systems. We have, so far, only seen the most simple of what will be infinitely complex and wonderful manifestations of the application of the Internet. Its evolution will be, from time to time and for some people, violent and frightful, but at other times it will be benign and will bring a lot of benefits.

The creative, imaginative and least fearful PR people are having a great time in this new era. The ones still wrestling with the fax machine or making the call to see if a journalist has received an e-mail are surviving as the last piece of inconsequential matter after an implosion that always follows a fiercely burning red star. The recent boom for the PR industry we know now is the red star; its imminent and sudden change will allow it to become the feedstock for something that is beyond our present dreams.

Have fun in cyberspace PR.

Index

page numbers in *italics* indicate figures